The Eden Design

CHRISTINA JARVIE

CROSS
BOOKS

CrossBooks™
1663 Liberty Drive
Bloomington, IN 47403
www.crossbooks.com
Phone: 1-866-879-0502

©2009 Christina Jarvie. All rights reserved.

No part of this book may be reproduced, stored in a retrieval system, or transmitted by any means without the written permission of the author.

First published by CrossBooks 11/19/2009

ISBN: 978-1-6150-7051-0 (sc)

Library of Congress Control Number: 2009941978

Printed in the United States of America
Bloomington, Indiana

This book is printed on acid-free paper.

Friends,

Welcome! You have chosen to embark on this journey with me and I am so glad that you have. Here we will learn all that God intended for our lives and what we can do to participate in his design.

Take time with each day of study; look up each of the verses so you don't miss what the Holy Spirit may have to say to you. Even if the verse is familiar the Lord can certainly show you something very fresh from it! As Hebrews 4:12 says "The word of God is living and active, sharper than any two edged sword."

Be honest with yourself and with God. I pray the very best for you as you venture into a discovery of God's grace and love.

Blessings,

Christina Jarvie

Contents

Week One
    The Designer   1

Week Two
    Design: Freedom   27

Week Three
    Design: Obedience   57

Week Four
    Design: Intimacy   81

Week Five
    Design: Fellowship   109

Week Six
    Design: Fulfillment   139

(Endnotes)   165

About the Author   167

WEEK ONE

The Designer

This week you will be learning about our Mighty Creator, the Designer. Who is He? What is He like? Why should I want to know Him?

Be prepared to open your heart to the Lord's design for your life, He'll blow your socks off!

Day One: The Eden Design

Day Two: Getting to Know the Designer

Day Three: The Designer's Benefits

Day Four: Jesus, The Sower

Day Five: On The Garden Path

Day One

The Eden Design

The Garden of Eden. Whether you are believer or not the idea of the garden of Eden conjures up a multitude of images. First there is the image of beauty and peace, the idea that life is easy. Next you might think about a place that felt like heaven, a place where God and man walked side by side. I know when I think about the garden of Eden I think of a place where I would have no worries; no grocery shopping because the food is right there, no laundry to do because – well, you know…and all the fighting and fear that infests a fallen world is non-existent.

God himself took the time to plan and design this place, this Eden, because he knew it would be the dwelling place of the people he would make. I am sure that it filled him with such delight as he spoke and fruit trees of all kinds came into being, perhaps he thought "oh these are so delicious, I bet they are going to love this!" You see, God has had a plan all along, since *before* the foundation of the world he knew the you would exist and he loved you already. In that love he designed a life that would be wonderful.

God has had a design for human life since the moment he breathed life into Adam's lungs. In fact, even before he spoke the words "Let there be light" he had a blueprint for life. Contrary to modern day ideas, God did not make the world and leave us to fend for ourselves. No, he created the world to be a paradise for man and to be a place where man and God had a perfect and complete relationship.

Our God created this world for man to participate in the abundant life he'd planned for man.

I am certain that you have heard the phrase abundant life many times before. Preacher's encourage you to pursue abundant life, books tell us that we should be living an abundant life, Jesus says that he has come to bring us abundant life. What has always eluded my understanding, however, is what does an abundant life look like?

Turn in your bible to John 10:10, what do *you* think it means to live an abundant life (some version say a full life)?

To have a better life because of Jesus + the promise of hope he brings

I would venture to say that the above question is impossible to answer unless you have a full knowledge of what God intended for life to be like before the fall. To find those answers we need to take a journey back in time before sin entered the world, we need to go back to the beginning.

Let's read Genesis chapters 2-3 in its entirety and then we will begin to dissect it.

Look again at the following verses from what you just read and answer this question for each: "What was God's design for life?"

Genesis 2:16-17 – *To do what is in our best interest and follow his instruction*

Genesis 2:18 – *To not be alone, to be able to share and help each other*

Genesis 2:22 – *To share/love, with another*

Genesis 2:25 – *see beyond physical w/ eyes*

Genesis 3:8 – *To always be open to him not to hide in shame*

4 | CHRISTINA JARVIE

Based on the verses above I believe that God's Eden Design for man can be summed up in the following categories:

Freedom   **Obedience**   **Intimacy** **Fellowship**   **Fulfillment**

Praise God, He created each of these designs to give us the very best, the highest blessings…a life lived abundantly!

The word "abundantly" in the original Greek means: <u>super abundant in quantity, superior in quality, exceeding abundantly above, beyond measure.</u>[1]

Can you honestly say that you live abundantly? Is your life superior in quality? Do you get excited to please God? Do you feel satisfied and fulfilled?

Hey, don't get discouraged if you wouldn't describe your life as abundant, the Lord our God is in the business of changing lives and you are a tablet that He would loved to write "abundant" all over!

You see, God created us to be satisfied in all that we do, whether it is working, going to school, or raising children. He created us to be familiar with who he is, to have an intimacy with Him that would delight our souls. God created us to have enjoyment and fulfillment through our relationship with him. We were created to help each other, to have companionship and to have perfect, unhindered fellowship with God.

We were also created with freewill, giving us the freedom to choose the kind of life we would like to lead; a life of abundance or a life designed by self, for self.

The Eden Design | 5

Which of the Designs above really speak to your heart, which of them gives you the chills to think you could live it in <u>abundance</u>?

Now, to address the first question of "what does it look like to have an abundant life", I want you to dream a little. Looking at God's design for life what would your life look like if lived in abundance. Since life is different for each person I would like to share with you what my abundant life would look like, and **then you write yours in the spaces below**:

As a stay-at-home mom I would take great pleasure in caring for my children all day long and I would never feel as though I wanted to hide in a closet rocking back and forth with a glazed over look in my eyes. I would also view the cleaning and maintaining of my home as a privilege and do it as "unto the Lord", rather than be angry when I find perfectly clean clothes in the dirty hamper and mashed up grapes on my freshly mopped floors (thus the rocking in the closet). I would love the taste and texture and smell of food rather than counting each calorie, fretting about rather this bite will sit on my waist when I am done eating it. I would enjoy summer because God creates each season, rather than glowering over the thermostat when it rises past 80 (which it is right now, 100 degrees to be exact). I would be thrilled to help my husband and encourage him in his work instead of resenting his coming home from work 20 minutes late. I would eagerly anticipate the times that I can spend talking with and learning from my Creator instead of viewing my quiet times as a required interference in my day, and I would be delighted to obey God all the time, in every circumstance.

<u>What would your life look like?</u>

Day Two

Getting to know the Designer

We will be taking a journey together over the next six weeks. On this journey you may be getting to know for the first time the life long adventure of our wonderful God, or perhaps you have been on this journey for a while. If you've known our Designer for a long time don't make the mistake of thinking that you have nothing left to learn; God is a trip that will never end. This journey will also be an excursion into the depths of our hearts; we will explore what we *really* believe about God, about the Bible, and about ourselves.

The ideas presented in the first lesson are big – really big. To imagine that God created human kind with the desire to give us abundant life in every area of our life, well, that is a big idea. It's hard to wrap my brain around the thought that I could have abundant – superb quality – life when I live in a fallen world.

It's difficult to believe that God created this world for anything other than what it has turned out to be; a world of death, mourning, and dissatisfaction.

I would wager to say that the idea is completely unbelievable – if you don't believe the character of the One who came up with the idea.

Here lies the fundamental problem through out the world: who really believes God? Who actually reads the Bible – God's word – and believes what it says?

Millions of people believe that God exists. Yet believing that God exists is futile if you don't believe who God is according to His word.

Dell Tackett of Focus on the Family's "Truth Project" poses this question: "Do you really believe that what you believe is really real?"

What about you? Do you live your life in a way that matches what you say you believe about God?

If you don't understand how to answer that last question, don't worry, we'll hash that one out over the next few weeks.

What I am trying to make clear to you is this: Our lives will not be changed, improved, or made better if we are approaching God as a self-help guru. God does not make our lives wonderful because we pay him to or because he feels obliged to do so. Our lives are changed because we know God. When we get to know God we desire to please him and when we please God our lives are changed, our families are changed, our marriages are changed. It all comes down to relationship; the purpose of our creation.

Turn in your Bibles to Psalm 139, Read it all the way through once and then answer the questions below:

What does God know about you? (vs.1-6)

What does that fact say about God?

Where can you go to hide from God? (vs. 7-12)

What does that fact say about God?

I *love* this Psalm. When I was 17 I was challenged to memorize this Psalm by a visiting summer missionary – Miss Eunice Perryman. Initially I memorized it for the prize of dinner out, but over the years it has become a great treasure chest of truth to me.

In this wonderful Psalm we can learn of who God is and how he feels about us:

1. He is Omniscient (all seeing).

> I can not go anywhere with out the eyes of God being upon me. He knows exactly where I am and what I am doing at all times. He knows my every thought, he knows each word that I am *thinking* about saying.

If you <u>believed</u> that God could see you all the time, and know each thought, would that change your life?

2. He is Omnipresent (all places, all the time.)

> Superman couldn't see through lead, so I could hide from him in a lead box. God, our Super Father, has no weaknesses, no limitations. Nothing can keep me from him. Nothing can keep him from seeing my deeds, not even darkness.

"Nothing in all creation is hidden from God's sight. Everything is uncovered and laid bare before the eyes of him to whom we must give account"

Hebrews 4:13

If you <u>believed</u> that God is with you, even in the darkest parts of your heart, would that change your life?

3. He made me on purpose.

   There is nothing quite as sad as hearing from a person that they were a mistake; that they have no purpose and they should never have been born. That is not what my Bible says, and that is not what I believe about God.

Psalm 139:13-16 tells us that God created us with intention. Write down the verbs in these verses that confirm God's intentional design:

Did you notice them? He created, he knit, he made, he wove, he saw, he ordained, he wrote. Oh, goose bumps. Don't you see how God our Father loves you?

I've tried weaving before, I have also tried crochet – which is akin to knitting – and let me tell you something; you don't knit something on accident. You approach knitting with a planned outcome and a purpose for the knitted object.

The Eden Design | 11

Sweet Girl, you have value, and you have purpose – and friend, you have a Creator who designed your life to be lived on purpose! You have the opportunity to have a deep abiding relationship with Almighty God, do you believe that?

If you really <u>believed</u> that you are able to have a fantastic relationship with our Father who loves you, would that change your life?

Each one of you will have a different answer for the questions above, but I hope that you have all come to understand that there is a difference between believing that God is up there somewhere and believing that God is involved in every part of your life and that He is crazy about you.

Day Three

The Benefits of the Designer

God has done so much in our lives, which is beautifully illustrated in Psalm 139. That God knows us and understands us so, and yet he still loves us? That is incredible. That he sees every attitude, every action, every misspoken word, each sin – yet he thinks about us and considers us a treasure. That is grace.

Since before you were born he has known you. He knew what you would look like, he knew what your character would be, he knows what delights your heart. Our loving God knows more about you than you know about yourself.

And still he loves you.

Does that thought stir a reaction from you? What is there about you that you think would be hard to love?

For me, I have a temper. I don't get easily angered, but once I am there look out! That is not a pretty part of me, yet it is a part of me that God is beginning to refine. I am not loveable when I am in a tizzy, and I stand amazed that even in those ugly times God still gazes on me with unconditional love.

Unconditional love – I would consider that a wonderful gift, and the Bible tells us that God has many benefits to offer *on top* of that love.

Read Psalm 103:1-5; here the Psalmist speaks of God's benefits, saying that we should not forget them. List those benefits below:

When I think of benefits my mind goes straight to the compensation one would get for working a job. I believe that if more Christians viewed the Lord God as their boss rather than a piggy bank to take from it would change their lives.

Our God *is* our boss, and he gives excellent benefits. Let's explore them!

He forgives our sin –

> This implies a continuous forgiveness. Thank you Jesus for forgiving my sin when you took them upon yourself on the cross. We must never forget that he continues to intercede on our behalf to the Father for the sins we continue to commit each day.

He heals Diseases –

> Our God is Jehovah Rapha – the Lord who heals. How many times have you been healed of a sickness? Do you know anyone who has been healed of cancer, or survived the physical pains of a car crash? Has God healed you from depression or anxiety. Let's never forget to thank him for his mercy.

He Redeems our life from the pit –

> This benefit you could say is a "biggie", who isn't grateful that Jesus has rescued us from hell? We are redeemed! We have been bought at a price; the high price of the blood of the Son of God. Strangely, sorrowfully, I know that we often forget this benefit. Wouldn't your life be different if you viewed each day from the stand point of having been saved from eternity in Hell?

He Crowns with love and compassion –

> There are character traits of Spirit-filled believers that unbelievers can not posses. There are times in my life that I *know* that I wouldn't have been able to love someone apart from the spirit within me! I am too judgmental on my own; oh thank you Lord that your Spirit crowns me with love and compassion.

Satisfies desires with good things –

Note the words "good things". Some of our desires, while altogether innocent, can reap disastrous results apart from God's will and intervention. Think of a single young woman who really desires a husband and family. Innocent desires, yes! What if, however, this woman were to rush in to a relationship that was outside of God's perfect plan for her life, outside of his timing? Disaster could happen. It's okay to desire good things but we must wait on God to deliver our desires, because he desires to satisfy!

He renews our youth –

Some of you may really love the idea of having your youth renewed, I know there are times in my day that I long for the energy and zest for life that my three young daughters have. The opposite of youth is a feeling of age – you're tired, you're weary. David recounts of time of hardship and weariness, saying "O God, you are my God, earnestly I seek you; my soul thirst for you, my body longs for you, in a dry and weary land where there is no water," and later he says 'because you are my help, I sing in the shadow of your wings. My soul clings to you, your right hand upholds me." (Psalm 63:1, 7-8)

We may be tired and weary but if we cling to God, our helper and our thirst-quencher, he will lift us in the shadow of his wings, upholds us with his hand and restore us.

Which of God's benefits seem especially meaningful to you right now, in this present season of your life? Why?

Notice that the Psalmist says to us "forget not his benefits". This verse stands out because we have such a history of forgetting what God has done in our lives! I know that I have. I have forgotten how he has saved me, and then it shows in how I act and live.

There was a group of people documented in the Bible who forgot the wondrous things their God and Savior had done for them.

Read Psalm 106:6-15, what was Israel's great sin?

Did you notice that "they gave no thought to your miracles, they did not remember your kindnesses"? Did you also notice that they "soon forgot what He had done and did not wait for His counsel"?

Amazing, isn't it, that this people had witnessed one miracle after another and soon forgot it happened! And when they forgot the benefits of God they began to doubt his power and they lost faith.

Think back to what great and mighty deeds God has done on your behalf. What are some God-sized miracles you've seen? Write them below, as many as you can think of:

My friend, you should never forget what God has done in your life, what he has done for your life. When we remember what God has done we can trust him more deeply when hard times come.

Spend the rest of your time in prayer, thanking God for who is he, for how much he loves you, and for His benefits.

Day Four

Jesus, The Sower

Jesus. The name above every name. The bread of life, the water of life, the Living Word of God. The Sower.

A sower is a person who is responsible for planting seeds. With out the seeds the fertility of the ground, the amount of water and fertilizer… well, it would all be good for nothing, A person may read the Bible, he may even go to church but without Jesus it is all an act of futility.

Oh, we need Jesus.

Today's lesson is simple yet it will require quite a bit of scripture hunting on your part. We are going to nail down today who Jesus is.

Now, before you skip to tomorrow's lesson because you think you've got the answer settled let me tell you why this is so important.

The Bible speaks at length about false religions, false gods, and false prophets. In our world we have plenty of those and without fail they all prove themselves as false by denying the deity of Christ.

I have personally experienced showdowns with the Jehovah's Witness religious group and ended up ashamed because I believed in Christ but I did not know how to defend his deity.

As Paul said in Philippians 3:10, "I want to know Christ and the power of his resurrection."

Ask yourself, can you really devote yourself to someone that you don't really know?

Okay, class, here is your assignment. Since popular opinion says that the old testament is supposed to be all about God and the new testament is all about Jesus; today we are going to draw lines from the old and new testament that will prove the deity of Christ.

Look up the verses and fill in the title given to God and Jesus from the verse.

God	Jesus
Psalms 75:7 Isaiah 33:22	2nd Timothy 4:8
Isaiah 44:6, 48:12	Revelation 22:12,13
Psalm 23:1	John 10:11
Isaiah 44:6 Daniel 4:37	Matthew 27:11 Revelation 19:16 1St Timothy 1:17
Isaiah 42:8 Exodus 34:6	1st Timothy 1:12
Isaiah 44:8	1st Corinthians 10:4
Isaiah 43:11, 49:26	1st John 4:14 John 4:42
Genesis 1:1 Isaiah 43:7	Colossians 1:16

There can be no denying that based on the word of God we can know for sure that Jesus is God. This knowledge can strengthen your faith and confirm within you that we serve a God who has died for us; a God who wants us to have life in abundance.

If you have doubted or put off recognizing Jesus as your Savior and King then now is the day of your salvation! Don't wait any longer. Ecclesiastes says that God put eternity into the hearts of men, so you know deep within that there is more to life than just you. There is Jesus, who paid the penalty of our sin to the Holy God who can not have a part of sin. Put your trust in Jesus, ask him to forgive your sins and tell him that you believe in Him as God, the Son, and you need his salvation.

Do it now. Eternity is waiting.

Day Five

On The Garden Path-

Walking on a holy path is a hard road to follow. It is easier to live as you please and it is easier to not bother yourself with holier pursuits. So why should we bother? Really, what is the point?

I can tell you that if I didn't have to have quiet times and Bible studies I might have the time to watch a show or finish the laundry. If I didn't have to go to church I might be able to sleep in on Sundays, have a leisurely brunch and get some yard work done.

So why is it that I carve out time for the Lord? Why is it that I choose a PG movie over a R rated movie?

The simple answer is Love.

Read 1st John 4:19. When you love someone what do you want to do with the person you love?

Everything! Spend time with them, get to know all about them; their likes, dislikes…You wish to emulate them, to do the things they like to do so to impress them. You express your love by giving your time, giving gifts and notes, and telling everyone you know all about your special someone.

What was it that caused you to love your first love?

When I met my husband I loved that he made me feel wanted and special, he liked being with me and he thought I was funny. I loved that he gave me something to look forward to; I felt he was the best part of me. In wanting to show the depth of our love we expressed warm words and did special things for each other. Ryan, through much practice, has become good at showing his love to me; for instance, one morning I woke to a heart shaped out of Cheerios on the top of my stove. It was a sweet greeting from the one my heart loves.

And God does the same. He shows us, each day, how He loves us!

So what did God do to show his love for us? Read 1st John 4:9-10 and answer below:

In response to God's gift to us, God's love and affection for us, it seems reasonable to assume that we should want to pursue him, to find out all about him, to brag on him to everyone around. We should be devoted to him because he is devoted to us!

What holds you back from complete devotion?

Is it hard to love Him because you can't see and touch him?

Can I make a rather disturbing statement? You can not really love God if you lack faith in God. Faith is believing in what you can not see and if you find it hard to be devoted to God it may not be a "love" issue, it may be a "faith" issue.

Think of someone who lacks faith. What is it that these people doubt?

If you lack faith in God; be it His sovereignty, his power, trust in his love or purpose for you, then how is it possible to love God and thereby have the desire to please him?

Fill in the following blanks from Hebrews 11:6:

> "And without _____ it is impossible to _____ God, because anyone who comes to him must believe that he _____ and the he rewards those who _____ seek him."

There are quite a few references in the gospel in which Jesus confronted people who had poor faith, little love, and still went through the motions, thinking they were bright stars in God's universe. Can you think of whom I am referring to?

Read through Matthew 15:8-9 and Luke 11:37-42. Who were these people and why were they offensive to Jesus?

The Eden Design | 23

1st Corinthians 13:1-3 sums it all up. Based on verse 2 what are you if you have no love?

What about you? Do you go through the motions of religious activity but find a certain passion, excitement, and desire for God seriously lacking?

Take a moment right now to ask God to rekindle a flame for Him.

Let's make a full circle; our initial question was "what's the point of walking a different path?" The answer is that obedience is our expression of love for God. The point of walking a different path by obeying God is because we love him and we want to express our love by obeying. Obedience. Obedience apart from love is nothing more than a clanging cymbal.

Read 1st John 5:1-5. According to verse 2 what are we to do?

God says in verse 3 that his commands are not burdensome. Now read Psalm 16:6, what are some examples of God's boundaries in your life?

The Lord has not given us commands to follow in order to choke us, not for a cosmic power struggle nor to be a "kill joy". He sets our boundaries to protect us, to bring us safety, and ultimately to bring us joy.

What would be some consequences for breaking the boundaries written above?

Read Matthew 22:36-40

Could you imagine living a life loving God with your entire being; heart, soul, and mind. Would you be capable of disregarding your boundaries if you loved God in that way?

So understanding that God's commands are not burdensome and that we are to love him completely how does Deuteronomy 30:19-20 fit all that we've discussed?

By choosing to love God, and choosing to obey his commands we are choosing life. Abundant life. Joyful life. Free Life.

Psalm 119:32
"I run in the path of your commands, for you have set my heart free."

WEEK TWO

Design: Freedom

This week we will begin to dig in to all the dynamics of the Eden design for our lives, beginning with freedom. We will see how our generous Lord has not made us clones, robots, or slaves. He has set us free, so what are we going to do with that freedom?

Day One: Free to Choose

Day Two: Free to Follow

Day Three: Free to Stand, part one

Day Four: Free to Stand, part two

Day Five: Free to Stand, part three

Day One

Free to Choose

Built in to the perfect design of our lives is freedom. No, I am not saying that everyone is born free, with an easy happy life to look forward to. Some of you know first hand that many are born into chains; the chains of an abusive family, the chains of poverty, the chains of racial inequality, or the chains of disability. Yet still we are born free!

The freedom that I am speaking of is the freedom of will. God has given us freewill. As part of his design he has allowed us to make choices with our lives: Spiritual choices. Despite our best attempts to convince ourselves otherwise we have made each and every sinful act out of sheer will.

It is very interesting to me that a Powerful, Eternal God would give us a free will. He could have created us, placed us at his feet and commanded that we love him completely. Nope, instead he has given us a choice; a choice between loving God, serving God and obeying God and the choice to not.

Why do you think God allows us to make the choice of committing our lives and love to him?

The heart of God wants to be loved by us. He loves us so wonderfully, and as our Father and Creator he wants to be loved in return. Yet, all though he *could* make us love him it wouldn't be a true love unless our will was engaged.

Oh yes, God wants us to *want to love him!!!*

And so he has given us choices. Will we choose to love and serve God or will we serve something else – or *someone else?*

I recently had a dear friend make a very poor decision that will change her life. Leading up to the decision this friend was very torn, deeply struggling with what to do. She knew that God's will was for her to not agree to this choice, but she continued to justify why she should do this thing. While wrestling with this choice she quoted to me from Joshua 1 "Choose you this day whom you will serve" and she recognized that choosing this thing would be choosing the World as her master, rather than God as her Master. Ultimately the world won out and her friends and church family sit back and shudder.

When we choose to follow the way of the world we are choosing to follow Satan's will. Read 2nd Timothy 2:26 and write the verse below.

Did you know that Satan LOVES it when we sin! He gets the mightiest knee slapping, belly laugh when we sin. He knows that our sin takes us captive to do his will. What a horrendous thought; that I would choose the ways of the world and cause Satan to dance a jig.

What does it mean to you when you read "the ways of the World"? What does the World represent to you?

The World is everything that is contrary to God. The Holy Spirit sets very clear boundaries here in the verses:

"Do **not** love the World or **anything** in the world. If **anyone** loves the world *the love of the Father is not in him*. For **everything** in the world – the cravings of sinful man, the lust of his eyes, and the boasting of what he has or does – comes **not** from the Father but from the World." 1st John 2:15 – 17

Clearly we have a side to choose, but not only to choose, we have a side to serve. Read again the verse you wrote above from 2nd Timothy 2:26. Satan desires to take us captive to do "His Will".

What is Satan's will for us, according to John 10:10?

His will is simple really. Satan, the god of this World, wants to steal and kill and destroy us.

He can't steal our salvation so he wants to steal our joy.

He can't kill our bodies so he tries to kill our spirit.

He can't destroy the power of our Savior, so he destroys our witness *for* our Savior.

Some kinda boss huh? Who would want to serve him, you may be asking yourself.

Now, take a look at your life. Is there something in your life that represents the world? Is there something in your attitudes, your choices or your words, which lump you in with the rest of the world. If there is, write these things below and confess them to God.

The Eden Design | 31

Read Ephesians 2:1-2, 4-5 in the margin.

Don't you just love God's rich mercy? Once dead in our sin now made *alive* in Christ Jesus. It is not the world that we should be following so hard after, Jesus our Savior is the one whom we should be serving!

Remember the friend whom I have referred to? She has allowed herself to be deceived. She believes that by choosing to run amok in the world will give her opportunities to witness and share God's love. As spiritual as this may seem the role that she will be playing will only serve to benefit Satan's side, and Satan has deceived her by wrapping a dark package with light.

> *Eph 2:1-2*
> *And you He made alive, who were dead in trespasses and sins, 2 in which you once walked according to the course of this world, according to the prince of the power of the air, the spirit who now works in the sons of disobedience,*
> *Eph 2:4-5 But God, who is rich in mercy, because of His great love with which He loved us, 5 even when we were dead in trespasses, made us alive together with Christ (by grace you have been saved), NKJV*

"And no wonder, for Satan himself masquerades as an angel of light"

2nd Corinthians 11:14.

Have you ever been deceived by our enemy? Has there been a time in which you convinced yourself you were doing something right when deep down inside you knew it was not God's will?

I was in a relationship that was ungodly but I was convinced it was God's will because he loved me and God wouldn't send someone in my life to love me if it wasn't His will, right? I was so very deceived.

We must never forget that we are in the middle of a cosmic battle and there only two sides from which to choose. God's or Satan's. That's it, there is no middle ground.

Finish by reading Ephesians 6:10 -13. I pray for you that when the day comes, when you have to make a hard decision that you will be able to stand.

Day Two

Free to Battle

As we begin let's recap what we discussed in our lesson from yesterday. God, in his gracious design for our lives has given us free will. He so desires for us to have a relationship with him; however he wants us to *want* to have a relationship with him. So we must make a choice. A daily choice of whom to serve.

Once we have made the decision of who we will serve it is then that we get to choose *if* we will follow. "Is there a difference?" you ask – indeed there is a big difference.

God has a purpose built in to each one of our lives. He has purposed us to have life, have it in abundance, and to have a relationship with him.

Think of the person to whom you have the best relationship. What about that person draws you to them, and what makes your relationship work?

I think of a woman in my church who has become to me like a mother. I can talk to her about anything and I trust the advice that she gives me because I have seen the integrity of her life line up with her words. In so many ways our relationship works because we are so similar – we have the same desire to know God and to pursue a close relationship with God. It is that like-mindedness that knits us together.

In God's pursuit of relationship with us he has offered us a wonderful gift. It is the gift of becoming like-minded to Christ Jesus. The more that we are like Jesus the closer we can become to kindred relationship with God.

Let me tie up some loose ends now. I stated previously that there is a difference between choosing to serve God and choosing to follow God.

Read Philippians 1:3-6, what did God begin in you and when will that work be complete?

If God began a good work in you, does that mean that you are a finished product right now?

                              Yes   No

If you are not a finished work that means that there is more work to do. Since God did not make us mindless robots could this imply that our <u>cooperation</u> is necessary in order for God's work in us to be complete?

                              Yes   No

We then have a choice to make, hmm? A choice that will determine what kind of work can be done in our lives leading toward our completion. Do you see the difference now? We may choose to serve God by not following the ways of the world, but if we don't go beyond that point and let him do the work of completion then we have not chosen to follow him.

God desires for us to be like our Lord, Jesus Christ; to be Christians, which means little Christ's. In Romans 8:28-29 our God says to us:

> *"And we know in all things God works for the good of those who love him, who have been called according to his purpose. For those God foreknew he also predestined to be <u>conformed to the likeness of his Son</u>…"*

Read Philippians 1:9-11; here Paul finishes the statement he began in verse 6 regarding our completion and what it would look like. In the space below write what the work of completion looks like in the life of a believer:

Can you say of yourself, right now, that your <u>love abounds in knowledge and insight</u>. Can you say that you are able to <u>discern what is best</u>, that you are <u>pure and blameless</u> and that you are <u>filled with the fruit of righteousness</u>?

Of myself I cannot truthfully say that I am any of those things. I can, however, say that I am being taught and am learning more and more all the time.

Is your relationship with God the same today as it was 2 years ago? Is it better, more mature, or has it become stalled? Why?

We are canvases, works of art in the process of being finished. Will we allow the painter to do his work on us or will we try to grab the brush from his hand and do the job ourselves?

Look again at Philippians 1:11, there is a tiny little word that will make the hugest difference in our lives written there. This little word is truly the key, can you see which word it is?

Through.

Abounding love comes <u>through</u> Jesus.

Discernment, purity and blamelessness come <u>through</u> Jesus.

The fruit of righteousness comes <u>through</u> Jesus.

With out Jesus we would have none of it, because in and of ourselves we do not have the capability! We Need Jesus.

We need Him, we need him, we need him.

We can not complete ourselves. All of these self-improvement, self-help books may give interesting insight into some issues that you are facing, or even give you tips about how to make things appear better but you can not be completed – perfected, made whole – apart from Christ. You need him, all else is striving.

Read Isaiah 55:1-3; God calls out to us with the answer to all of our striving for that one thing that will satisfy, what is his solution?

Come to me, listen to me, hear me! Oh, I need my Savior. You need him too.

I hope that you have made the choice to serve our Lord God instead of serving the world. Now, as I write this I am praying for you that you will see that you need to follow Christ and allow God to transform you into the likeness of Christ, and in doing so you are choosing life.

Finish by reading Isaiah 55:11-13, enjoy this beautiful picture of a life that is abundant.

Day Three

Free to Stand

<u>The Armor of God, Part 1</u>

Have you made your choice? Have you decided which side you want to serve yet? Oh, I hope that you have. Let's transition now to another freedom that God has given to us as part of the Eden Design. The freedom to stand.

We are at war and God is ready to empower us to fight this war and to be fully equipped for this war. So how are we to be armed to come into the battle field? Actually, I guess the real thing to ponder is "since I am already in this battlefield then how can I begin to battle victoriously?"

The Lord has not left us powerless in this dark world, praise God, He does have a defense system armed and ready! We will be spending a lot of time learning about God's defense system for us, in fact the rest of this week will be devoted to this defense system.

Remembering of course that this study draws parallels between the Almighty's design in the Garden of Eden and our lives I thought it completely appropriate and personal to draw some parallels between gardening and the Armor of God. Those of you who hate gardening just hang with me as best as possible.

So let's begin…

Turn to Ephesians 6:10-19 and list below what Paul calls the Armor of God.

Now look back through those verses again. How many times is the word "Stand" written in this passage?

When a single word is used a number of times in one passage let that word get your attention. The Holy Spirit has something big to say here and he uses the word "stand" a lot.

The context of this passage puts us in the midst of a spiritual battle that goes on in all levels of creation. On earth, in the heavenlies, and all places in between there are battles going on for the hearts and minds of all men, women and children. God does not want us to go through the battles only to come out at the end crawling and bloody. He wants us to come out of these spiritual battles with our hands on our hips, our heads held high and standing tall! The Holy Spirit's mention of standing so many times can lead us to believe that he will also equip us to stand!

My friend, you are a warrior. God wants to arm you with the weapons of war.

The Tool Belt…the Belt of Truth

When I am going to tackle some serious weeding in my garden I want to come prepared with all of my tools: My trowel, my shovel, my gloves, my pruning shears. Seriously, I am lazy, so I know that if I get down on my knees and begin to dig away only to realize that I have forgotten something I will look across the yard to my garage and have absolutely no desire to get up and go get the forgotten object.

I must prepare, in advance, my tool belt and have it with me when I tackle the weeds.

I *know* I will be facing a task, I *know* the work of pulling weeds is waiting for me. I don't want to come unprepared.

Read again verse 13 of Ephesians 6, fill in the missing words:

> Therefore put on the full armor of God, so that _____ the day of evil comes, you may be able to _____, and after you have done everything, to _____"

Now read 1st Peter 5:8-9.

> **"Be self-controlled and alert. Your enemy the devil prowls around like a roaring lion looking for someone to devour. Resist him, standing firm in the faith.."**

What is your gut reaction to verses such as these?

It is scary for me to know that there is an evil out there looking for me and wanting to destroy me. It is also scary to know that it is not a question of "if" it is a question of "when". Knowing these truths it would be foolish of me to walk into the battleground of this present darkness unprepared.

So we snap on the tool belt of truth. It is the belt of preparedness. It is the belt of readiness.

What is in the tool belt?

The Word of God
Accountability
Prayer

<u>Work Clothes…the Breastplate of Righteousness</u>

When I prepare myself for working out in the yard I wear my old tennis shoes, my grubby jeans, and a shirt that is okay to get dirty in. I realize that the process of fighting the weeds is a dirty job so I dress accordingly.

In scripture the choice of clothing for particular events and duties was meticulously chosen and recorded. For instance the Holy Spirit goes into great detail about the garments that the priests were to wear.

Exodus 39

> *"From the blue and purple and scarlet yarn they made woven garments for ministering in the sanctuary…they made the ephod of gold, blue, purple and scarlet yarn, and of finely twisted linen…they made shoulder pieces for the ephod which were attached to two of its corners…they fashioned the breast piece…then they mounted four rows of precious stones on it.…"*

In 2nd Samuel 6 when David is escorting the Ark of God back to Jerusalem the Bible records him as wearing a linen ephod, or fine clothing. On the other hand the book of Matthew records the clothes that John the Baptist wore.

Read Matthew 3: 4, what does the Bible record John as wearing?

Sounds kind of itchy to me, but again he was dressed prepared to preach repentance to the backslidden Israelites in the desert. So how does this relate to the armor of God? Let's tie all the ends together.

Turn to Revelation 19:7-8, what does the fine linen of the Saints stand for?

Conversely, read Revelation 16:15 – what is it that we wish to avoid by having our clothes with us?

Now read Revelation 3:17 below:

> *"You say, 'I am rich; I have acquired wealth and do not need a thing.' But you do not realize that you are wretched, pitiful, poor, blind and naked."*

Clothing tells those around you a lot about yourself. Are you feminine, hip, sporty or casual? Do you take care in your appearance? In the same way our spiritual dress (our righteous acts) tells God a lot about your heart.

If the righteous acts of the saints were recorded as fine linen then it would be fair to say that those who were naked and ashamed were seriously lacking righteous acts.

Isaiah 58 describes some righteous acts that God encourages and desires from his people. As you read the verses below circle those acts:

> *"Is is not to share your food with the hungry and to provide the poor wanderer with shelter – when you see the naked, to clothe him, and not to turn away from your own flesh and blood…then your righteousness will go before you, and the glory of the Lord will be your rear guard" 58:7-8*

God created us to do good works (Eph 2:10), and He wants us to take care of those in need (James 1:27).

We need the armor provided by the Holy Spirit if we are to stand firm in the midst of the corruption of the world which means if we are neglecting our <u>quiet times of prayer and Bible study, neglecting the local church body, and neglecting our involvement in ministry and service</u> we will be unprepared for battle and an easy target for the enemy.

Tomorrow we will continue with the armor of God. For now, in the space below, examine your heart and ask yourself "if Jesus were to return tonight would I be found to be dressed in my fine linen or would I be found naked and ashamed."

Day Four

Free to Stand

Part Two

This is heavy stuff. Man, it sure would be nice to be able to just kick our feet up and not concern ourselves with all this battlefield/enemy on the prowl stuff. Unfortunately we know full well by now that we do have an enemy who wants to destroy us and that the battles, the opposition to our following Christ will come. Naiveté is only cute in kids, but to be naïve now would only cause us ruin – so though you may be tired let's call on the power of the Holy Spirit and press on!

> *"If you have raced with men on foot and they have worn you out, how can you compete with horses? If you stumble in safe country, how will you manage in the thickets by the Jordan?*

Look back at your lesson from yesterday and summarize below how the Belt of Truth and the Breastplate of Righteousness will arm you.

Wear Work Shoes - Feet fitted with the Gospel

Read Jeremiah 12:5 in the margin; what do you think God is trying to say to us in this verse?

Something that I hope will become clear to us throughout our journey this week is that <u>we are told to be prepared.</u> We have been given directions through the Bible, and a tour guide through the Holy Spirit in order to navigate our way through the spiritual battle field that is this world.

Why don't we use it??

I must be prepared; I am not going to wear flip flops or high heels when I go out to dig in my garden. I am going to be prepared with shoes that are appropriate for dirty work.

In Jeremiah 12:5 God says to Jeremiah "If you stumble in safe country, how will you manage in the thickets by the Jordan?" In the same way, if you haven't readied yourself for battle when times are good, how can you expect to survive during times of warfare?

Have you ever been through spiritual warfare? What did the warfare look like?

I have had times when I was very afraid. After having my first daughter I had nearly paralyzing fear that someone was going to kidnap her, or hurt her. I have had times going downstairs in my darkened house and I would sense something that made me fearful. On one occasion I had walked across the hall to use the restroom, it was all dark in the house except the light in my bedroom my husband was reading by. As I crossed the hallway I was broadsided by a sudden and intense fear; I felt like I was being watched. Now normally I would have run into my room and hidden under the covers and prayed. This time, however, I stood in my hallway and looked out into my darkened living room and the sense that I had was that I was staring into the eyes of a demonic presence. And I stood firm. *Then* I ran and hid under the covers. After catching my breath I told my husband what had just happened and we prayed, and prayed. And God comforted me and it is my belief that he covered our house that night with his mighty angelic warriors.

You see, spiritual warfare doesn't always come with burning crosses in the front yard or mistreatment by neighbors who know you are a Christian. In whatever form it has come to you or will come to you the point is that it will come. And readiness is important.

When you are wearing your shoes that are "fitted with the readiness that comes from the gospel of peace" you can be bold to step out into the thickets.

Sunscreen – the Shield of Faith

Read again Ephesians 6:16, what can we extinguish with the shield of faith?

I have compared the shield of faith to sunscreen for several reasons. First, the purpose of sunscreen is to deflect the harmful UV rays of the sun, it doesn't keep us from getting hot but it helps protects us from being burned.

Faith is similar. Faith will protect us from being mortally wounded from arrows of our adversary, that doesn't mean that we aren't going to feel the heat of the attack.

Let's visit again the Parable of the Sower. Read Matthew 13:5-6, what was it that scorched the plants and made them wither?

In the explanation of the parable Jesus says that the sun scorched plant had no root and when trouble and persecution came this plant fell away. Many Christians who have recently come to faith in Jesus are taught that when you become a believer then life is daisies and sparkling cider from that point on.

That is not what the Bible teaches.

Remember, we have an enemy who hates us, who hates the power that lives in us in the form of the Holy Spirit, and he will do anything to quench that power in us.

Now regarding trouble and persecution; from which some fall away from faith, let's be mindful that sometimes sunburns happen when you aren't aware. Sometimes you spend the day in your garden and hours later you begin to feel the ache of the burn. Had you been prepared you would have thought to put some sunscreen on right? Compromise is like that, it is when we look back at our difficulties we say "if only".

When we compromise on issues of obedience it is the same thing as "forgetting" to put on sunscreen. What is an area in your life where you can be prone to compromise?

For me it is what I put before my eyes; sometimes "forgetting" – though in truth I do know – that what goes into my eyes gets stuck in my head, and then comes out through my mouth. Ouch.

I pray that we may never be caught unaware when Satan turns the heat of compromise on in that way.

We must daily apply faith just as we daily apply sunscreen.

Read Colossians 2:6-7 below, circle all the verbs in these verses (the action words):

> *"So then, just as you received Christ Jesus as Lord, continue to live in him, rooted and built up in him, strengthened in the faith as you were taught, and overflowing with thankfulness."*

Did you notice the responsibilities that Paul is commending us to follow through with *after* the point of our salvation?

You continue, **you** be rooted and built up, **you** strengthen your faith, **you** be thankful.

Just as in Ephesians 6 Paul says to take up the shield of faith, the silent command is "**you** take up that shield." This will require work, this will require trusting the Lord all the while.

> *"Now faith is being sure of what we hope for and certain of what we do not see."* Hebrews 11:1

What does faith mean to you?

I believe the answer is found in verse 6 of Hebrews 11, write that verse below:

God says that we must believe that he exists (is) and that we should earnestly seek him. If we believe that God is who he says he is, which requires us to root our selves in his word, than we will know that the hardships we will face are under his control.

My friend, we can only know these things about God when **we take up our faith as a shield to protect us from the attacks of the enemy.** Don't let yourself get burned.

Day Five

Free to Stand

Part Three

As we have explored the armor of God, the work clothes that we must put on in order stand against our enemy I hope that you have not had a sense of defeat. Sometimes there seems like there is so much to *do*.

Instead I hope that you have begun to feel like Xena, Warrior Princess. You have been smacked around by Satan and now it is time to stand up, strap on your armor and fight.

> *"For God did not give us a spirit of timidity, but a spirit of power, of love and of self-discipline."*
>
> *2nd Timothy 1:7*

At this point, how are you feeling? Defeated or Ready to get some business done? Why?

As we draw near to being completely outfitted with our work clothes let's be reminded of each piece we are to put on.

Belt of Truth – our tool belt that is filled with the tools necessary to equip us for God's work.

Breastplate of Righteousness – the appropriate clothes to get dirty in, stands for the righteous acts that ready us for service (Bible study, quiet time, prayer, ministry).

Feet Fitted with the Gospel – wear your work shoes; we have readied ourselves so we can step out into the harder times without fear.

Shield of Faith – Put your sunscreen on; we apply faith by knowing who God is and that we can trust him when our enemy turns on the heat.

Which of these pieces of clothing seems hardest for you to put on?

<u>The Helmet of Salvation – A Wide Brimmed Hat</u>

The purpose of a wide brimmed hat, besides being really cute, is to protect the ears and the eyes from the heat of the sun.

Did you know that most people who remember to wear sunscreen often forget to put sunscreen on their ears? That's right; a lot of people are walking around with sunburned ears. Left continually unprotected those sensitive areas; the back of the neck, the ears, and the eyes, could lead to skin cancer. Skin cancer takes you by surprise; in fact "skin cancer is the most common form of cancer in the United States. More than 500,000 new cases are reported each year – and the incidence is rising faster than any other type of cancer"[2]

I had a teacher in high school; he was also my track and field coach. We kids would often tease him for his choice of clothing while out at practice because he would come wearing long sleeve shirts, long pants, and a wide brimmed hat. He would dress like that even on really hot spring days. You see, our teacher had had skin cancer on the back of his neck when he was younger and he knew that it was his exposure to the sun that had caused his cancer. He was being very careful to not let that happen again; he was sensitive to his risk and he came prepared.

We Christians have all had cancer too. Spiritual cancer. When we were saved by the grace of our Lord Jesus Christ he healed that cancer in us. Yet so many of us have returned unprotected to the very things that we should be sensitive to.

The eyes and the ears are the in valve to the mind and it is from our mind that we make the choice to sin. So when we choose to put the armor on our head we are choosing to shelter our minds from what goes into it via our eyes and ears.

Like my teacher we should all be sensitive to the areas in our life that can cause destruction.

I know full well that I have sinful tendencies in particular areas, so the choice I have to make is *am I going to expose myself to that or not?*

Be very honest with yourself, what are your areas of greatest temptation to sin? Are you going to continue to expose yourself to it?

I have a very vivid imagination. Pair that with a teenage life style of reading romance novels like they were going out of style and you have a woman with lots of lust on her mind. Knowing that about myself I also know that putting my eyes on movies that promote lust and sexual ideologies will lead my thought life right down the drain. If I want to please the Lord why would I revisit those desolate places?

God wants us to have freedom; Read Galatians 5:1 and write this important verse below:

Again a choice must be made. The Lord desires our freedom, he desires us to be able to stand –don't you think it would be terribly hard to stand with the weight of a yoke upon your shoulders?

Put on the helmet of Salvation – protect your mind by shielding your eyes and your ears.

The Sword of the Spirit – The Fly Swatter

There is nothing worse than the sound of a buzzing yellow jacket in your ear. The fear that accompanies that sound is borne since early childhood, since you first were stung. This tiny little pest sends grown men running, arms flailing, shrieking like a girl (yes, I have personally seen it).

It is hard to be brave against an oncoming wasp if you have no protection, isn't it? However, when you have come prepared to your garden with a sturdy flyswatter in hand you feel a bit more sure.

Jesus was assaulted by one such pest, and yes he was prepared.

Read Matthew 4:1-11, how did Jesus defend himself against the stings of the enemy?

Did you see? He was prepared with the word of God, the Sword of the Spirit. To each temptation Jesus replied – not with logic or argument – but with the power of God's word.

Jesus is our example! Just as he faced the enemy of freedom with the word, so too should we!

Notice that Jesus was at his weakest point when Satan came to tempt him. Matthew 4:2 says that "*after* fasting forty days and night…the tempter came." Satan comes to us in our weakness too.

When do you feel spiritually weak? Have you been weak lately?

Let me point out one thing more….Jesus knew his Bible. He was prepared for this temptation ahead of time.

Read Psalm 119:9-11 in the margin, then answer this: what are we to do with God's word, why?

"How can a young man keep his way pure? By living according to your word. I seek you with all my heart; do not let me stray from your commands. I have hidden your word in my heart that I might not sin against you."

When the hornet buzzes in your ear a tempting thing, a sinful thing, it is our sin nature trying to place us again under the yoke of slavery.

From reading 1st Corinthians 10:13 and James 1:13-15 what can we learn about temptation?

Always remember that our Designer has a plan for freedom. We must *fight* for our freedom, we are in a spiritual battle and there can only be one victor.

Attacks are coming, be prepared! Prepare yourself by reading and knowing God's word. Trust his word when you face hard decisions, know his word when you meet an unbeliever, live his word daily as a righteous saint of God. And pray.

Then, girl, you stand!

WEEK THREE

Design: Obedience

Following God in obedience is the foundation of our walk with the Designer. If we refuse to be obedient then ultimately we refuse to have a right relationship with the Lord. Take your time with God this week to examine yourself, examine your life, and watch what the Lord will show you!

Day One: Owning up to Obedience

Day Two: Understanding Obedience

Day Three: Repenting of Disobedience

Day Four: Lukewarm Obedience

Day Five: Blessed Obedience

Day One

Owning Up to Obedience

It was simple really. "Do not eat from the tree that is in the center of the garden…" It was a choice given from a Loving God who desires our freedom.

It was God's one rule, his only law, and Adam and Eve chose to disobey.

Adam and Eve had sinned grievously against God. Eve desired more than she had been given and disobeyed God's command to not eat from the tree. The irony of it all is that Eve gambled with and lost all of the things that we wish we had: security, purpose, an easy life, and perfect fellowship with God.

In response to their sin God allowed the consequences for the sin that Adam and Eve had committed. They were told that they would have death if they ate from the tree- and indeed they did.

You see, our desire is to have life; a joy-filled life of purpose, and when we sin, our sin brings death. Physical death, relational death, and spiritual death.

God handles sin in his people in one of two ways. Read 1st Corinthians 11:31-32 in the margin and see if you can identify the two methods of correction:

1.

2.

1. **God disciplines his children**

    The KJV says that he chastens us. Chasten means "to afflict in order to reclaim"[3]. God loves us so much that he will not let us stay where we are, in sin, in complacency. So he will afflict us in order to bring us back into his fold.

Read Hebrews 12:5-6, 11. What is your initial reaction to these verses?

It was not until I began raising children that I began to understand these words. In order to keep my children safe I give them boundaries (you may not run out into the street), I teach them respect by not allowing them to get sassy with me (soap anyone?), and in order to show them that willful disobedience has consequences they are indeed disciplined!

In the same way God gives us boundaries and he will allow us to endure the consequences for violating those boundaries.

Can you think of an example of a consequence for sin that God will allow?

I worked at a summer camp the summer before my senior year in high school. While there I met a young man and fell madly in like. Though we weren't supposed to, this young man and I snuck out of our respective cabins after curfew and went on a walk. Shortly into stolen moments the camp manager – our boss – found us and we were sent to bed. Now, sneaking out may not seem like a big deal but at the onset of our summer the rules were clearly laid down one being that curfews were strictly enforced. Normally we would have been fired, this summer however they were terribly understaffed and they couldn't afford to send us home, so instead we were grounded. When we weren't working we were to be in our cabins – for a whole week. It was agony! Worse, it was a consequence for sin.

2. **God allows us to discipline ourselves**

Remember what 1st Corinthians 11:31 said, "but if we judge ourselves we would not come under judgment." The basic meaning of this statement can be summed up with three simple words:

Acknowledge   *Confess*   *Repent*

We acknowledge (judge) that our actions or thoughts were sinful based on the conviction of the Holy Spirit. We confess that we have sinned in this manner. We repent (feel grieved) of our sin and ask the Lord to "keep me from willful sin" (Psalm 19:13)

God is so holy that each time we sin it is an offense to him and it is truly a thing of loving-kindness that he does not treat us as our sins deserve to be treated. He is so loving to allow us to discipline ourselves!

Discipline; this word has always been interesting to me. In today's view the word discipline is often accompanied by visions of bared hineys and wooden spoons. The word <u>can</u> mean punishment but it also means: "training, to train up well, teach".[4]

Read Titus 2:12, what is it that the word teaches us to do?

Now read 1st Corinthians 9:24-27. To what does Paul compare his spiritual training?

Notice that Paul says a competitor goes into strict training. It is with such a mindset that we must discipline ourselves to obey God, thus bringing Him glory.

You cannot separate the act of judging yourself and the act of training yourself. A runner must train to run in a race because he knows that he has no chance of winning unless he trained. In the same way we must train ourselves to say no to ungodliness, first by recognizing within ourselves that ungodliness is indeed present.

Go back to Genesis 3:9-13, Did Adam and Eve take ownership of their sin?

What did they do instead?

Adam and Eve both blame-shifted their sin. The old "devil made me do it" adage apparently began in the garden. I have often wondered if they would have owned up to their sin and repented right away if they would have received as severe a punishment as was given them. In the process of training ourselves to be a competitor in Jesus' corner you must judge yourself, you must take ownership of your sins.

Day Two

Understanding Obedience

The life of a follower of Christ is a safe and wonderful place to be. I am praying that you are learning to embrace this God-made design in your life and understanding that before God can move on in our lives to bring us fulfillment and joy and purpose we must do our part in following Him in obedience.

Yesterday we addressed the opportunity God gives us to discipline ourselves and to judge our lives. We are learning that we must train aggressively to bring our sins and strongholds to God's altar and to leave them there.

We learned that disciplining ourselves can be summed up into three words. What are those three words?

_____   _____   _____

Do you really want to have a full and abundant life? Do you really want to have a life that God can bless and use for His glory? I know I do! I want all that God offers me; I want fulfillment, contentment and every other *ment* there is! My sweet friend the Lord stands waiting for the opportunity to enrich your life and give you meaning, but a life that is crowded with sin does not have room for the things of God.

If you are serious about pursuing God you have to set your mind to these things:

1. **Listen to the Holy Spirit**

    Only the Holy Spirit can convict of sin, teach and guide us, yet a life that is impeded by ungodliness can turn a deaf ear to the Spirit and limit the power that he could have displayed in your life. 1ˢᵗ Thessalonians 5:19 says "do not quench the Holy Spirit" which implies that we have the ability to limit his power if we live a lifestyle that pursues the things of this world.

Let's look at a real life example of someone who tuned out conviction. Read 2nd Samuel 11: 1-27, what shows evidence that David was unaffected by conviction?

Did you notice that Bathsheba went through the entire pregnancy clear through the birth of a son with out David repenting of his crimes? So, we're looking at the better part of a year without repentance and with broken fellowship between David and God – he being a man after God's own heart!

2. **Put a Definition on your Sin**

It is very easy to cast off feelings of conviction if you can gloss over the seriousness of your sin with "soft" words or definitions of what sin is. For instance fornication is sin; it means to have sexual relation apart from marriage. Since our current social conscience considers intercourse as the interpretation of sexual relations many people delude themselves into believing they are not sinning if they do everything *besides* intercourse. This is a very serious deception!

What are other ways believers gloss over their sin?

Justify it, blame it, give it other names. For instance, how many times have you shouted, "I am so frustrated!" when what you really are is filled with anger. You must examine if you are righteously angry or are you angry because something is not going your way?

Read Colossians 3:5-10, list the sins that we are to put to death below.

1.
2.
3.
4.
5.
6.
7.
8.
9.
10.
11.
12.

Now go back and give each a definition, use your dictionary if you need help.

Did you recognize something of yourself in any of the definitions listed above? How does that make you feel?

So…if you patted yourself on the back thinking you skated past that list unscathed remember the words of 1st John 1:8, *"If we claim to be without sin we deceive ourselves and the truth is not in us."*

3. **Get Specific**

   Modern day words detour us from classifying our action and thoughts as sinful. We do disservice to our Savior and the Holy Spirit when we are convicted and then shrug off the convictions based on not finding "our sin" listed in the Bible.

   In the spaces below, fill in the blank with the true definition based on the sins you just defined above.

   1. Tell a dirty joke   _____

   2. Scream at someone who cuts you off   _____

   3. Exaggerate a story to make it funnier   _____

   4. Read lusty novels   _____

   5. Gossip about your in-laws   _____

My friend, it is very easy and comfortable to allow yourself to think you are doing good in the whole "sin life" arena; you're not having an affair, you haven't killed anyone, you're not a thief – so surely God must think you're doing pretty good, right?

Our Father God says "all (your) righteous acts are like filthy rags" (Isaiah 64:6); even on our best days we can't hold a candle to God's holiness.

We are all infected by our sin nature and we must not let ourselves be deluded into thinking otherwise. I say this not to make you feel defeated but to inspire you to change your life, acknowledge your sins, so that your life will glorify God rather than hide his glory.

The Eden Design

Day Three

Repenting of Disobedience

In Psalm 51 David begins the process of restoration with God over his sins of adultery and murder. Read this Psalm all the way through.

Based on the tone of David's words, I can imagine that David was face down before the altar of God; eyes streaming with tears, body wracked with sobs, nose dripping like a faucet. Confession is not a pretty sight, but I believe that God finds it a thing of beauty.

Write verse 17 of Psalm 51 below:

This verse is a picture of confession and repentance.

In the original languages the meaning of confession is:

> *To assent, acknowledge, agree fully, profess, promise, bemoan (with wringing of the hands). Revere, worship (with extended hands)*[5]

I love how expressive these words are because it illustrates the whole self being involved in confession.

A sad fact about confession is that many people believe that it is the end point. If they confess a sin and get forgiveness they can feel better about themselves knowing they have fulfilled their end of the "bargain".

I once saw a movie in which a group of girlfriends were leaving church and one of the girls said, "I love Sundays! I get to wipe my slate clean and think about how to dirty it up again tomorrow!"

What a sad state of the heart.

When we confess our sins to God we are agreeing with him that we know we committed these sins – it is not a surprise to God. Yet confession is the starting point of reconciling ourselves to God. It is by no means the end point.

As John the Baptist always proclaimed…"Repent!!"

Turn to 1st Kings 8:46-50, can you identify three different ways God refers to repentance in these verses?

The original languages describe repentance as:

> *To think differently, reconsider, to sigh, breathe strongly, to be sorry, to turn back, not necessarily with the idea of return to the starting point.6*

My favorite of these definitions is *"to turn back, not necessarily with the idea of return to the starting point."*

Repentance is stopping the sin you have been committing and choosing to not do it again! I used to swear like a sailor but the Lord showed me the sin of my mouth and I repented of it, now when I hear swearing it is like nails on a chalkboard!

Have you ever experienced true repentance? Celebrate in the lines below, from where has God brought you?

Look again at Psalm 51:17, what words does David use to describe repentance?

Have you ever known someone who has broken a bone? I have heard stories of broken legs that were healing crookedly so the doctors had to rebreak the bone, set it correctly and let it heal properly. What a beautiful picture of God's love!

Despite our best attempts at "straight living", we are helplessly crooked, but when God gets hold of our crookedness he "breaks" us, and then sets us straight so we can heal.

Repentance hurts. It is painful. It is hard to handle. But my friend, repentance sets us free!

Read John 8:34 and 2nd Peter 2:19 and paraphrase them below.

What, or who, has mastered you?

2nd Timothy 2: 26 says "..and escape from the trap of the devil, who has taken them captive to do his will."

If you remember from the lesson titled "Free to Choose" we know that it is Satan's will for us to sin! He loves it when we sin. He loves it when we *think* we have the right to choose to sin because that makes us *free*!

No, on the contrary, when we choose to sin we are choosing enslavement. 2nd Timothy 2:25 says that repentance leads us to the truth. What is that truth…it is the truth that Satan wants us enslaved!

The truth of Satan's battle strategy is why four paragraphs later in 2nd Timothy 4:7 Paul says "I have fought the good fight.."

We are in a fight, we are at war! Satan desires to make us ineffective and weak, and then he can cripple our witness for Christ and put us on the sidelines by keeping us captive to sin.

Jesus wants us free, and he gives us freedom from sin through confession and repentance!

Is there something holding you back? Is there something in your life that you know, deep down, that you have failed to repent of, turning from it fully? If there is now is the day of your freedom!

Lay it down girl! Lay it down!

Day Four

Lukewarm Obedience

In the middle of writing this Bible study I received terrible news. My father had died very suddenly from a massive heart attack. One moment he stood at the stern of his brand new motor boat and the next he lay lifeless. Thus began my cross country journey from Washington State to Atlanta Georgia.

As I prepared to leave my thoughts and prayers were not on "oh God, how could you have allowed this to happen", instead I prayed "Oh God how will you receive glory through this?" and I continued to pray that God would use me in any way necessary to bring him glory and to bring my family comfort. I knew also that my friends and church family were praying for me; that I would speak truth to whomever God would have me encounter.

The Lord certainly answered our prayers.

Rev 3:15-16
15 'I know your deeds, that you are neither cold nor hot; I wish that you were cold or hot. 16 'So because you are lukewarm, and neither hot nor cold, I will spit you out of My mouth

I had an opportunity to speak truth to 2 men on 2 different flights, I was able to speak truth to a cousin I had never met, an aunt who is not saved, and to others who came to visit the family to share their grief.

Through all the interactions something began to be startlingly clear to me; a common thread ran between most of these individuals. That common thread was the comfortable life they had made for themselves in the "grey zone".

Read Revelation 3:15-16; what is the charge that Jesus is bringing against the church of Laodicea?

What do you suppose it means to be lukewarm?

Have you ever had lukewarm milk? Disgusting isn't it? If I am going to have milk it either has to be very cold or it has to be hot, with foam, espresso, and dark chocolate in it. (Mocha anyone?). Seriously, can you understand the words of Jesus when he said "because you are lukewarm…I will spit you out of my mouth."

With that in mind look at the words below; each of the words are synonyms for the word lukewarm. Circle the word(s) if they represent you in your present day walk with our Lord:

Unenthusiastic	Half Hearted	Indifferent	Apathetic
Tepid	Cool	Unexcited	Subdued

Could you imagine if Jesus felt indifferent or half-hearted toward you?

Jesus does not mince words when he says how he feels about our being lukewarm toward him, read again Revelation 3:16, what will he do to the lukewarm?

Lest you get a wrong impression this verse by no means insinuates that Jesus will rescind our salvation. This is a loss of intimacy, a loss of fellowship – a loss of what we were created to have and need.

Turn now to Isaiah 59:2 and write the verse below:

Is there anything in this verse that seems disturbing to you?

Our sin separates us, our lukewarm living separates us. Yes, sweet friend, if you are compromising your values, if you are blending in with the world, you are a lukewarm believer.

Let's begin now to distinguish between hot and cold. Read the following verses and write what it is that a "hot" person would be like.

1st Peter 2:9

1st Peter 4:1-2

1st John 2:3-6

An unredeemed person does not have the ability within themselves to become hot – not apart from knowing Christ. All those things that characterize an on fire believer, well, the opposite would hold true for the cold.

Read 2nd Timothy 3:1-5 to get a sense of the cold side. Do you know anyone who fits into the description of these cold people?

Here's an alarming question: do you know a person who claims to be a follower of Christ that fit into this description?

The very sad thing about the era in which we live is that Christians are indeed living their lives as though they are not really believers. The truth is that they live to please themselves knowing that they have been saved and they are not going to hell. The great delusion is that Satan has convinced us that it is okay to live this way!

It is <u>not</u> okay to live this way! God has created us for so much more than mediocrity and lukewarm living. Do not let yourself be suckered into believing that you can live as you please and still live abundantly!

Paul addresses this issue in 2 Timothy 4:1-4. Have you ever believed mainstream hype because it suited your desires at the time?

Yes   No

As a friend said recently, "Christians want a salad bar religion, they want to be able to pick and choose based on what suits them." One of the men that I met on the plane trip to Georgia was a man who had recently been saved. A man who was homosexual and adamantly defended his homosexuality – even to the misquoting of scripture. Though this man is saved his life still had the stench of hell on him because he was unwilling to give up the comfort of his sin.

Read Matthew 23:37-38, fill in the lines below:

O Jerusalem, Jerusalem, you who kill the prophets and stone those sent to you, how often I have longed to gather your children together, as a hen gathers her chicks under her wings, _____. Look, your house is left to you _____."

Can you hear the pain and longing in the voice of our Savior. He longs for relationship, he longs for us to be whole. <u>Fill your name in the space below</u> and read the modern day version of Jesus' longing.

O _____, _____, you who ignore my word and avoid the truth, how often I have longed to teach you, protect you, and nurture you, as a mother does to her children, but you were not willing. Look, your life is left unfulfilled and wanting.

I titled this lesson Lukewarm Obedience. But really, lukewarm obedience is not obedience at all.

Day Five

Blessed Obedience

All this week we have explored the design of obedience, yet perhaps you have noticed that we have learned more from the direction of what obedience is *not*. Long ago I had a conversation with my mentor regarding the instruction of parental respect; this had been a challenging time with a spirited 2 year old daughter who was really pushing buttons and becoming disrespectful toward me. In learning how to reach my daughter I was told to teach her what not-to-do and then reinforce with praise those things she ought to do. My friend told me that people often learn best what something is by understanding what it is not.

For four days we have addressed what obedience is not. We have also learned what the consequences are for living a life of disobedience: loss of fellowship, loss of intimacy, and enslavement to sin.

I am excited that we can now turn our attention to what obedience *is* and what the rewards for obedience are.

Throughout the course of this study our lives will be affected by who we believe God to be, and what we believe is his character. In a life of obedient living we must always remember that God wants us to obey him because of his great, great love for us.

Turn to John 10 and read verses 1-15 then answer the questions below:

What does Jesus refer to himself as?

From vs. 3-4, how do the sheep respond to the Shepherd?

What does the Shepherd do for the sheep, based on verses 7-15?

It is no big secret that sheep are often considered dumb animals, but one thing that *is* going for them is that they do recognize the voice of their shepherd and will respond to his voice by following him. Now, the role of the shepherd was to protect and care for his sheep – it was the shepherd who would lead them to new pasture land for food, it was the shepherd who would take them to water, and it was the shepherd who would place his sheep in pens at night to keep them safe from robbers and predators.

Normally a sheep does not feel inclined to say to himself, "Ya know, it looks like the grass is getting a bit thin here. I think we ought to move on down the lane a bit and get some new grass." <u>He is completely dependant on the Shepherd for his care and protection.</u>

What then would happen if the shepherd were lazy and unconcerned for the welfare of his sheep?

Surely the sheep would fall victim to starvation and death.

Jesus calls himself the Good Shepherd, and twice he says that he lays his life down for his sheep.

What does that mean to you, that Jesus is the Good Shepherd?

I feel well taken care of under the care of the Good Shepherd. Praise you Lord! If you get a chance read Psalm 23 to get a better grasp on the Good Shepherd.

Suppose one of the sheep decides to make a break for it. Maybe he thinks this whole "sheep pen" idea is for the *really* dumb sheep and that he can handle whatever may come. He knows kung-fu; he can totally take that wolf...

So, he jumps the fence when he thinks the Shepherd isn't looking and off he goes.

The Parable of the Lost Son exemplifies perfectly one who thought he would be better of without the care and protection of his "Shepherd".

Read Luke 15:11-20. What happened to the son after he left that care and protection?

My friend, whether you like it or not we have been placed within a pen and yes, we have been given boundaries. Yet those boundaries are not there to steal our joy or to enslave us, our boundaries are there to keep us safe!

As Israel was preparing to enter the Promised Land Moses gave instructions from God as to the boundaries they were to remain within.

Read Deuteronomy 30:15-18 in the margin; what was commanded of Israel?

Deut 30:15-19; 15 "See, I have set before you today life and prosperity, and death and adversity; 16 in that I command you today to love the Lord your God, to walk in His ways and to keep His commandments and His statutes and His judgments, that you may live and multiply, and that the Lord your God may bless you in the land where you are entering to possess it. 17 "But if your heart turns away and you will not obey, but are drawn away and worship other gods and serve them, 18 I declare to you today that you shall surely perish. You will not prolong your days in the land where you are crossing the Jordan to enter and possess it. NASU

Israel had a clear choice – obey the Lord and have life and prosperity or disobey and have death and destruction.

We have the same choice.

How does it make you feel to know that you have boundaries? Do you feel angry and powerless? Do you feel protected and sheltered? Explain your thoughts below.

I know the story of a man who wanted to live his life without boundaries. He wanted to taste life and enjoy life to the hilt! So, expecting the best enjoyment could be found in women and boozing and material possessions this man set about to conquer every woman, drink every kind of alcohol and buy the very best possessions regardless of its affordability. It was all the best for him!

Some time later this same man hit the very lowest of low. He found himself diseased, broke, indebted, and lonely. Some life huh?

I know the story of a man who found Jesus. Who learned that Jesus had set boundaries to protect his heart, to protect his body, and to protect his well-being. He followed Jesus, learned to listen to his voice and he learned that the enjoyment of life was in getting to know his savior.

These men are one in the same, and his life was changed when he decided that his boundaries were pleasant.

Jesus said that he came to give us life to the full, and fullness comes as a result of obedience.

Yes, Jesus is our Good Shepherd; our protector, our provider, our caretaker. And he offers us so much, but he can't bless our lives if we refuse his Shepherding.

Examine your heart, my friend. Have you refused to obey the voice of the Lord in a particular area of your life because you think you can take care of yourself? Do you really think you know better than God?

In Psalm 16:2 David says, "I said to the Lord, 'You are my Lord; apart from you I have no good thing.'"

Do you believe it?

WEEK FOUR

Design: Intimacy

Each human, at their deepest level, is a human looking for a connected and meaningful relationship. This week we can begin to see how Jesus Christ has made himself available to us as the most intimate of friends. I hope you will enjoy learning what a kind and loving God we have the privilege of relationship with.

Day One:	A Picture of Intimacy
Day Two:	Wasted Intimacy
Day Three:	Intimacy through Prayer
Day Four:	Intimacy through Study
Day Five:	Intimacy through Accountability

Day One

A picture of Intimacy

There is a grand old tale that tells of a hard pressed young woman and the man who swept in to save the day. It is the first of its kind really, this Knight in Shining Armor story that fills the hearts of each little girl. We all want that knight to rescue us, to save us from the dread beast, and to carry us off to his shining castle.

It is a longing for intimacy, to have our hearts flutter with anticipation as our knight on horseback rides in to save the day. Why do you think there is story after story, and movie after movie that embodies our deep desire for rescue?

Because that is the way that God made us.

Oh yes, he made us to desire a savior.

The story of Ruth tells a tale of a hard pressed young woman, and the man who swept in to save the day. This woman is a picture of us, the church, and the man – well he is a picture of our Savior, Jesus Christ.

Begin by reading the story of Ruth. If you have time read all four chapters in the book of Ruth, and allow yourself to look at the story with new eyes.

First we have Ruth – the damsel in distress.

Ruth was a widow and a foreigner among the Israelites, she came from the people groups whom Israel was to avoid and be separate from. Ruth had no children, in fact she may have been barren given the fact that "after they had lived there ten years, both Mahlon and Kilion died" (verse 4). Being a widow is awful, but a barren widow…basically this means that she had no standing as a person of value in her society.

We know that Ruth and Naomi were poor, having to pick up the scraps the harvesters left behind. We can also infer that Ruth had very little hope for an outrageously happy life and that Naomi had become bitter.

All these facts set up the idea of poor Ruth; poor, barren, helpless and alone with bitter company.

Next we have the hero, Boaz.

Read Ruth 2:1-4. What do these verses tell us about Boaz?

Can you just picture Boaz, riding astride a gleaming white horse, as he greets his workers, "The Lord be with you!" and they all stop what they are doing to wave a hand of greeting to their favored master, "The Lord bless you!".

Doesn't it just capture your imagination?

Then his eyes light upon a young woman, bent over and sweating under the hot sun. He inquires after her and he realizes something… she is needy.

Based on chapter two of Ruth, summarize what Boaz kindly does for Ruth.

Yes, Boaz knows that Ruth is needy. He also knows that he can provide for her, that he can meet her needs.

That is just like our favored master, the Lord Jesus. He knows that we are needy and he knows that he can meet those needs.

Can you see how, preceding salvation, we are like Ruth?

- **We are poor.**

That doesn't necessarily mean poor monetarily! We are spiritually poor. In Revelation 3:17 Jesus says of the church of Laodicea, "You say 'I am rich; I have acquired great wealth and do not need a thing.' But you do not realize that you are wretched, pitiful, poor, blind and naked."

Yes, we are poor. Without a Savior our souls are bankrupt.

- **We are hopeless.**

My friends, you must realize the bleakness of our situation. There is no candy coating the knowledge that without a Knight in Shining Armor we have no hope of a hopeful future.

Read Revelation 20:11-15 below and underline what will happen to those who names are not written in the book of life.

> 11 Then I saw a great white throne and Him who sat upon it, from whose presence earth and heaven fled away, and no place was found for them. 12 And I saw the dead, the great and the small, standing before the throne, and books were opened; and another book was opened, which is the book of life; and the dead were judged from the things which were written in the books, according to their deeds. 13 And the sea gave up the dead which were in it, and death and Hades gave up the dead which were in them; and they were judged, every one of them according to their deeds. 14 Then death and Hades were thrown into the lake of fire. This is the second death, the lake of fire. 15 And if anyone's name was not found written in the book of life, he was thrown into the lake of fire. (NASU)

Hell is a terrible reality, but we who have trusted Jesus for our salvation have nothing to fear. This free gift from our knight in shining armor is available to everyone! "If you confess with your mouth Jesus as Lord, and believe in your heart that God raised him from the dead then you will be saved"! (Romans 10:9)

- **We are barren.**

What do you think it means to be barren?

You may remember from a previous lesson my freakish need for consuming water; hold on I need to get a drink...there is nothing more sad to me then getting thirsty, grabbing a cup previously filled with water, tipping it back in eager anticipation and then! Nothing. It's empty. That's what I think of when I ponder the meaning of being barren; there is so much hope followed by crushing disappointment. There is so much need for those who are barren – whether it takes on a physical, emotional or spiritual form. Boaz knew that Ruth was needy and empty, he also knew that he had the way to fill that need. Jesus tells us that he knows the way to fill our needs too.

> *"Remain in me, and I will remain in you. No branch can bear fruit by itself; it must remain in the vine. Neither can you bear fruit unless you remain in me."*
>
> John 14:4

Go back to the verse above and circle the word that Jesus uses repeatedly.

This word "Remain" in the Greek is "Meno" which means "to stay (in a given place, state, relation or expectancy):-abide, continue, dwell, endure, be present, remain, stand, tarry (for)."[7]

Jesus tells us that he knows our needs, and he can meet our needs, our deep desire for intimacy – but it is *we* who must remain with *him*. He is not going to chase us down yelling "No, come back! I want to meet your deepest inner longings! Please, come back!"

Ruth understood this about her hero; she knew that in order to be rescued she must humble herself and *ask* to be rescued.

Now let's see the happy ending between Ruth and Boaz. Read Ruth 3 & 4, answer the questions below.

What did Ruth do to Boaz?

How did Boaz respond?

What was the happy ending?

Ruth understood her needfulness and she knew that Boaz was the answer to that need. So she went to him with her need and he responded with joy! What an intimate moment it must have been between our maiden and our hero. My friend, can you see how you can have that intimacy with our Savior? We must realize that we have a need, and we must go to him and lay at his feet!

What is your need? What do you need to lay down at the feet of Jesus?

Jesus and Boaz are heroes. Boaz was the hero to Ruth, and by extension to Naomi; he rode in to save the day.

Jesus is the hero to every living being on this earth. The Bible speaks of a day of rescue, when our hero will ride in to save the day:

> *I saw heaven standing open and there before me was a white horse, whose rider is called Faithful and True. With justice he judges and makes war. His eyes are like blazing fire, and on his head are many crowns. He has a name written on him that no one knows but he himself. He is dressed in a robe dipped in blood, and his name is the Word of God…on his robe and on his thigh he has this name written: King of Kings and Lord of Lords."*
>
> *Revelation 19:11-13, 16*

Oh, I can't wait!

Day Two

Wasted Intimacy

Yesterday we enjoyed the sweet beginnings of an intimacy between ourselves and our Lord Jesus. Today we will see the opposite of this relationship as the life of a believer refuses this relationship because of misperceptions,

Begin today's lesson by reading the Parable of the Minas in Luke 19:11-26. Before you read, however, understand that in this passage all mentions of "servants" are referring to those who are believers in Christ.

In ancient times the position of a servant was considered to be a position of great responsibility and privilege. Remove from your mind the solemn and ignored servants of Victorian era movies like "Pride and Prejudice"; instead look at the following examples.

Nehemiah (Nehemiah 2:1-8) A wine taster was in an interesting position because they did not simply bring the king his drink; they would first sip it in the presence of the king to test if there was poison in the drink, then they would serve it. Yeah, I don't think I would be standing in line for that job! However, in this place of honor as the cupbearer to the king of Persia Nehemiah was in a unique position to make a request to the king.

Joseph's former cellmate (Gen. 41:9-14) Again we have a cupbearer, this time to the pharaoh! Did you notice that the pharaoh had been addressing all his wise men and magicians when the cupbearer spoke up; I find that interesting because the Bible does not give the impression that the pharaoh was looking for the advice of a servant, yet take the advice pharaoh did!

Did you see the common thread between both of the servants? Each bore the privilege of having the ear of the king. They shared with the king and the king listened and responded favorably to their words.

I most love the example of Nehemiah, how the king noticed his face was downcast and that he was sad. Though being sad before the king of Persia could have been punishable by death, depending on the shifting moods of the king, we can know for certain that our sadness before the King of kings will never go unnoticed, nor will it ever be punished!

Let's circle back to the third servant of Luke 19. This servant was given a task, "put this money to work until I come back" (vs13) The servant was disobedient and did not do as his master commanded.

Not only did the servant choose to disobey the orders of his master, he began a character assassination!

What did he say about the Master, regarding his character?

Imagine the disappointment the Master had towards his servant; the servant that he had allowed close to him, the servant that he had listened to and cared about.

Have you ever questioned God's character? In other words have you ever experienced something difficult and said to yourself "Why is God doing this to me, doesn't he love me? Doesn't God want what is best for me? How could a God that is supposed to be good let this happen?"

Yes   No

Talk about blame-shifting, the servant laid blame for his disobedience on the master saying that he feared him and thought he was a meany..

Though I make light of his statement the reality is that he responded to God in a way that went against God's design. God designed us for intimacy. An intimate, connected relationship between mankind and God.

How is it, do you suppose, that the servant of Luke 19 had such a twisted view of his Master?

Maybe the servant thought he deserved more than one little mina to work with and since he didn't receive more he became bitter.

Maybe he didn't take his Master very seriously and supposed nothing bad would happen if he lived as he pleased while his master was gone.

Maybe things had gone wrong after he left and the servant felt abandoned.

Look back at the question that you answered regarding God's character and dig deeper – go beyond the yes or no. How has your heart responded to God when something has gone wrong? How have you felt towards him?

I had to admit to myself, after a hard season and a lot of prayer, that I did not trust God as he is worthy to be trusted. After a heart-breaking miscarriage God showed me that I had never trusted him with my other children and after he allowed this miscarriage to happen He taught me a valuable lesson on believing in His sovereignty and trusting in his purposes that I would not at the time be able to understand. It had all come back to the question of what I believed about God's character.

So what does the word of God tell us about God's character?

Look up the following scripture and write down the description of his character:

Jeremiah 31:3 _____

Jeremiah 29:12 _____

Exodus 34:6-7 _____

Oh sweet friend, don't you think it's time to get to know your God? Don't you want to know this Creator who is compassionate and forgiving; our Almighty Designer who is crazy in love with you?

I hope that you were reminded that God is approachable, compassionate, forgiving, and hugely loving. When we meet tomorrow I hope we can continue to unravel the mystery who God is and how we can have a deeper intimacy with him.

Day Three

Intimacy through Prayer

When my husband and I were newly dating I began to advocate that we would have prayer times together. I would tell him that prayer between loved ones was a very intimate thing to do. It is during prayer that you get to hear the heart of the other; it is during prayer that you hear the concern, the joy, and the heartache from your loved one that you might not be able to hear otherwise. Of course, because we were dating and completely infatuated with each other having our heads together and holding hands was a nice bonus.

I believe that God views prayer in a like manner. When we sincerely pray to him we are having a conversation of the most intimate nature. We are expressing our love, our shame, our concerns and our needs. We are placing ourselves in the care of the most nurturing of Fathers.

In return, it is often through prayer that God speaks back! Since a relationship can't be intimate and be one-sided I am so glad that God speaks.

Our job is to learn how to listen.

Let's review a very well known story in which God revealed to his prophet how it is that he speaks to us. Read 1st Kings 19:9-13, in what manner did God speak?

I, for one, am glad that God whispers gently. Were he to speak to me in the power of his might I am sure I would fall out of my chair!

Think about that! If God were always to present himself to us, his children, as a fearful booming volcano or an violent earthquake would we not quiver before him rather than approach him as our loving, intimate Father?

Don't get me wrong – God is the Almighty and fearful Lord and we would do well to remember that. It is his grace that allows us to come to him as a gentle shepherd.

> *"Therefore, since we are receiving a kingdom that cannot be shaken, let us be thankful, and so worship God acceptably with reverence and awe, for our "God is a consuming fire."'*
> *Hebrews 12:28*

What is prayer to you?

Prayer, in it's original language means:

- **To pray, intervene, mediate, judge**
- **Interceding for, prayer in behalf of**
- **To Make a request**
- **An asking, entreaty, supplication**[8]

I think that some people have the idea that praying to God is like removing money from the ATM machine. You ask for what you want, and in a timely manner you get it. Perhaps you feel some appreciation to the machine, but since it is only performing its function than not too much gratitude is necessary.

Here's an example of an ATM prayer:

"Dear Heavenly Father, thank you for this day, thank you for the sunshine, please forgive my sins. Please help me with (this), (this) and (this). Please do (this) for (them). Please do, do and do. Amen"

Have your prayers ever sounded like this? Yes or No

Do you think a lifestyle of intimacy with God is possible if he is nothing more than a means to an end? What then shall we do, after all sometimes we *are* in a season of life when we desperately need God to do and do and do!

I believe this is where praise makes all the difference.

It is when we praise God that we take the focus from ourselves, our wants, our needs – and we focus on God.

Read Psalm 150:1-2, read it out loud if you are able.

If only we would remember how little we are, and how big he is, I think that our prayers would take on a whole new meaning. We would know that God is approachable and loving; but we would also remember to treat him with reverence and respect!

David understood this.

Read Psalm 34 and answer the following questions:

How does David begin his psalm? _____
_____

Who does the angel camp around? _____
_____

Those who fear the Lord lack _____
_____

The Lord is attentive to whom? _____
_____

Who is the Lord close to? _____
_____

When we pray to our Lord we attune our hearts to him and we place ourselves in the position that God designed for our lives. He intended that we come to him as little children (Matthew 19:14) and he intended that we have the relationship that places us under his watch care. This is why Jesus refers to himself as the good shepherd who *takes care* of the sheep! It is a relationship between Father and child; trusting, secure, and intimate.

I have a friend who, at one time, I had been very close with. We were in one another's weddings, and we cared for each other deeply. Then time took its toll, and different lives separated us. Our friendship was not a priority anymore and it slipped quietly away. Now this friend is more of a memory and we haven't spoken in a very long time.

We did not have a falling out, we did not hurt each other's feelings – we just quit talking.

How can <u>not</u> talking to God cause the same effect as a neglected friendship?

When we choose –yes, choose! – not to talk to God we communicate quite loudly that he is not a priority and that we don't need him. I believe this breaks the heart of God who, unlike my friend and I, is never too busy to make you a priority.

Ahab is an example of someone who tried to manage his life without God. He was one of the most wicked kings of Israel and in the face of war, despite wise council, he chose to seek popular opinion and follow his own desires. He did go to war and was killed.

Now read a very different story of someone who prayed. Read 2nd Chronicles 20; write verse 12 below.

Prayerlessness leads to self-sufficiency which leads to bad decisions. I think Ahab learned the hard way that the advice of friends is not a good replacement for prayer.

Prayerfulness leads to dependency on God which leads to:

- **Strength – "Stand firm…"**
- **Hope – "You will not have to fight.."**
- **Faith – "See the deliverance…"**

I hope that you will see the intimacy that we can have between ourselves and our Lord when we have a healthy prayer life. Make it your priority to not neglect this friendship.

Day Four

Intimacy through Studying God's Word

In high school I had a long distance boyfriend; a young man that I had met while working the summer at a Christian camp. This was of course before the age of e-mail and internet chat rooms and blogging so we wrote letters to each other. I still think there is nothing greater than receiving a hand written letter in the mail box.

I remember finding these letters in the mail and feeling overcome with excitement; I would hug the letter to my chest and take it into the house, so very anxious to read it, but I wanted to have my privacy so as not to be distracted from his honeyed words. Ahh…

Then I would pour over every letter, I would read into the subtext of his sentences and I would eek out every bit of affection and love I could; why, even the "how are you?" line must have had a deeper meaning, right?

I loved his letters.

The Word of God is a love letter to you. A love letter that took thousands of years and dozens of writers; inspired by the Spirit of God. Within the pages of our Gardener's love letter we find so much affection, so many hopes, so much longing for us by the Father. Oh Jesus loves me, the Bible tells me so.

> "The Lord appeared to us in the past, saying 'I have loved you with an everlasting love; I have drawn you with loving-kindness."
>
> Jeremiah 31:3

> "For God so loved the world that he gave his only begotten Son, that who ever believes in Him will not perish but have everlasting life."
>
> John 3:16

> *"As the Father has loved me, so I have loved you. Now remain in my love."*
>
> *John 15:9*

> *"I in them, and you in me. May they be brought to complete unity to let the world know that you sent me and have loved them even as you have loved me."*
>
> *John 17:23*

Do you really believe that God loves you? It is easy to say "Jesus loves me this I know" but do you sincerely believe that he loves you?

I love my children. I *love* them! I stare at them in amazement as they grow, I plead with the Lord to allow me the privilege of watching them grow all the way up; I shudder at the thought of losing them…I would die for my children. *I love them.*

Yet I am merely human. I am selfish in nature and impatient and stirred to irritation more than I would care to admit.

Then there is God the Father who *loves* his son. He is a million times more capable of love than I am so I can barely fathom the love that he must feel for Jesus.

Jesus says that he loves us the same way Father God loves him.

Does that evoke any emotions or thoughts about how Jesus really feels about you? Record your thoughts in the spaces below:

So how is it that I know these intimate details about the love of the Father to us? How is it that the intimacy God communicated to us in the Bible has made its ways to the pages of this study book?

Because I am learning to study God's word.

Just as I studied the letters from an old boyfriend, I have come to love to study the letters of the Designer. If you want to become more intimate with the Lord consider these questions:

How often do you read God's word?

How much time do you spend in the pages of the Bible?

Do you feel as though you need to know God more?

My friend, we all need to know God more! We all need to spend more time in the pages of the Bible! God is infinite, indescribable, uncontainable, unfathomable. We will never understand him fully until we have met him face to face in Heaven.

But girl, I can tell you one thing, I am not going to waste my life choosing to not get to know him the best that I possibly can right now on this Earth…because when I do meet him face to face I want to recognize him as the one that I knew intimately from his love letters to me.

In your opinion, is there a difference between studying the Bible and reading the Bible?

Yes   **No**

Proverbs 25:2 says, "It is the glory of God to conceal a matter; to search out a matter is the glory of kings."

God's word has the same message from beginning to end. You will find Jesus from Genesis to Revelation. You will find your purpose, God's plans, the direction the world will go, and the practical insights into everyday living from Genesis to Revelation. You will not, however, find the "all you ever need to know about the bible for dummies" section in the Bible. You will have to search it out!

It is a treasure hunt. Can I just tell you; there's nothing more exciting than to find the answer to a question from the book of Hebrews in the book of Exodus! The Bible is the coolest book ever.

Read James 1:21-25, write verse 25 below:

The word "look" means to "to bend aside, lean over (so as to peer within), look (into), stoop down."[9]

This verse is conveying to us the idea that we ought not just take a glance, we are to lean over and check it out. We should dig into the treasure chest with both hands to see all the way down to the bottom. Only there <u>is</u> no bottom.

That is the beauty of God's word – it is unfathomable.

There was a season in my Christian walk when my husband and I were growing discontent with our former church – we weren't hearing the depth of the word and we weren't growing at all. As Ryan and I discussed what we could do about this stunted growth pattern he suggested that we start making time in our day for a quiet time. I, having attended a Christian college for two years in which I took a year long course reading through the Old and New Testaments, said "I don't need to have a quiet time, I have already read the Bible and know what I need to know."

What an Idiot!

Now, years later, I understand that there is so much that I need to know and that I still don't know. Praise God for his mercy.

We will not know Jesus apart from reading over and again his love letters to us. As I learn to study God's word I increasingly have an appreciation for the genius of God, for the organized nature of God, for his wisdom and His amazing love for me, oh I love him so!

Would you like to know how to study? Here's a real quick intro:

Arm yourself with a concordance – I use Strong's concordance which includes the Hebrew and Greek dictionaries. Next, pick a topic and look up that topical word in the concordance. List the verses and look up those verses in the Bible, take plenty of notes.

Now, pray and ask how that topic and those verses can be applied to your life. You will be amazed at what the Holy Spirit can reveal to a willing heart…a heart yearning for intimacy.

Day Five

Intimacy through Accountability

I hope through this last week you have come to desire and hunger for a deeper and more intimate relationship with our Designer. He loves you so much and wants the best life for you; that you "may be able to comprehend with all the saints what is the width and length and depth and height - to know the love of Christ which passes knowledge; that you may be filled with all the fullness of God." (Eph 3:18-19 NKJV)

God allows us to discover intimacy with him, but it is so important that we make an intimate relationship with God our priority! God has given us the tools to discover who he is and to understand him, but we must be proactive in the process.

As we learned last week, we need to be prepared for the spiritual battles ahead. We need to be clothed with God's word and have at the ready our tool belt. To be clear, spiritual battles are not just the times we are being persecuted; they are the times we are tempted to sin, the times we are around carnal people, they are the times when we just don't "feel" like going to church or having our quiet times.

It's time that put the last tool in our tool belt. So far we've loaded up with prayer, we've geared up with studying the scriptures and now we get to add in the very sharp tool of accountability. Accountability is a very important tool necessary for growing in intimacy with our Lord and that tool can be found only in the body of believers.

Paul instructs us how we are to relate to each other, read the following scripture and identify what he tells us to do:

Hebrews 3:13, 10:25

Ephesians 4:29

James 5:16

Galatians 6:2

I am convinced that God did not place us on this planet for the sole purpose of hoofing it alone. You can see through the whole of scripture that God has placed his saints together. With the exception of the times that God intends to do a major work on the spirit of his Saint, they have all been partnered together for the purpose of encouragement, support, and accountability.

Think back through some well known Bible stories and give some names of people who were partnered together. I will give you one example:

Adam and Eve

Why do you think we need accountability?

Proverbs 27:17 says this: "Iron sharpens iron, so one man sharpens another" and we also see that "two are better than one because they have a good return for their labor. For if either of them falls, the one will lift up his companion. But woe to the one who falls when there is not another to lift him up." (Eccl 4:9-11, NASU) The Holy Spirit is speaking very loudly here, do you hear what he is saying? You can't do this thing alone!

There is another aspect of accountability here that stretches us into a look at eternity. I believe that being held accountable to someone is a picture of the accountability that we will have to our Lord Jesus when he returns to earth as judge.

Turn to Ezekiel 8: 6-13, here is a vision that Ezekiel was given of the Elders of Israel who had deluded themselves into believing something, what was it they believed?

John 3:19-21 says:

> "This is the verdict: Light has come into the world, but men loved darkness rather than the light because their deeds were evil. Everyone who does evil hates the light, and will not come into the light for fear that his deeds will be exposed. But whoever lives by the truth comes into the light, so that it may be seen plainly that what he has done has been done through God."

<u>The truth is if you are serious about being rid of sin in your life you must bring into the light all of your deeds done in darkness. Don't deceive yourself into believing that the deeds that are unseen by the people around you are unseen by God.</u>

Read Hebrews 4:13 and Revelation 3:17 in the margin and write below the underlying theme of the two verses.

Heb 4:13, 13 And there is no creature hidden from His sight, but all things are naked and open to the eyes of Him to whom we must give account. NKJV

Rev 3:15-16, 15 "I know your works, that you are neither cold nor hot. I could wish you were cold or hot. 16 So then, because you are lukewarm, and neither cold nor hot, I will vomit you out of My mouth. NKJV

"Everything is open and laid bare",
"But you do not realize that you are wretched, pitiful, poor, blind and naked". To me, these verses are saying don't you know that God can see your deeds, that he knows your heart, and that you will be accountable.

God is omnipresent, he is with us at all times, and he is with us when we commit our secret sins, and when we think our secret thoughts.

When Jesus returns we will be called into account for all these things there were not brought to light.

Let's look and see where that is found in scripture. Turn to 1ˢᵗ Corinthians 4:5 and write that verse below:

Knowing now that we will be accountable, do you see now the value of an accountability partner? This partner, whose qualifications we will discuss, can help encourage us to not participate in sin; this person can challenge us when our walk with God stalls. Besides, there is something very powerful about revealing to someone in the flesh a thing that is spiritual; I think it defuses the allure of it a bit.

I just saw a cartoon today of a little boy who wanted to play at the junkyard, he thought he would find all sorts of neat treasures there. Upon asking his parents they strictly forbade him from playing at the junkyard because it was unsafe and he could get hurt. Well, this little boy disobeyed and snuck off to the dump and, of course, he got hurt. He cut his leg on a piece of scrap metal and scurried home, hiding in the garage. He was wounded, he was bleeding, but he did not want his disobedience to be found out. Along came his little sister who eventually convinced him to tell on himself to his parents so that his wound could be treated. Had he not fessed up and been treated he could have incurred all manner of infections. The healing process was painful (aka a tetanus shot) and being grounded, but he was saved from worse circumstances by his pesky little sister.

Can you see the metaphor here? God gives us commands to obey so that we will be safe, when we disobey we give ourselves wounds, if we don't confess those sins our wounds fester and become infected, and if we have someone come along side us they can help us see the wisdom of bringing our wounds to the Great Physician and we can be healed. When we learn to give all of our wounds, our temptations, our struggles and desires over to God we begin to find a certain intimacy develop.

When looking for an accountability partner, from experience and observation, this is what I perceive is what you should seek out:

Older/Wiser than you – reference Titus 2:3-4

> This person should have been down the road a bit. Perhaps you are a young mother struggling with anger at your children. If you had another mother with grown kids she can certainly pull from her bag of experience to encourage you. Now, don't assume this person will be the best partner simply because she is older. This leads me to the next requirement.

Walks with God – reference 1st John 2:15-16

> This person should not simply go to church, or maybe even teach Sunday school. This person should have a reputation for being in love with Jesus. Love for God should dominate her life; if you hear this person talking coarsely or gossiping this is not so.

Does not share your <u>present</u> struggle –

> This is very important! If you are in the same stage of struggle, temptation and stronghold as your accountability partner than neither of you will help the other. This is not to say that this person has never fought your same battle. This is saying that they should have had victory over this particular sin.

I have a dear friend who struggled with sexual immorality. When a boyfriend would come along, despite her best intentions she would often fall into sin with him. On several occasions she asked close friends to hold her accountable to the standard of purity she *wanted* to achieve in her relationship but these friends let her down big time. They did not ask her how she was doing; they did not ask her what she was doing. When my friend would bring up that she had fallen into sin they would sort of shrug it off. The friends were not accountability partner material. They were the same age, they were too close of friends to "risk" losing a friendship over it, and they weren't wise or godly enough to offer the counsel or the rebuking that was necessary.

If you are operating as the person keeping someone else accountable than you must remember that you will not do your partner/mentee any good by babying them in their struggles. Keep in mind that "faithful are the wounds of a friend." (proverbs 27:6)

I hope that you have determined to set about the task of finding an accountability partner. You can grow tremendously under the tutelage of wise counsel. If you need suggestions or help in locating a partner ask your pastor or Bible study teacher who they would recommend… and pray!

WEEK FIVE

Design: Fellowship

What an amazing adventure we get to go on together. In learning about God's design for humanity we have been taught more about the character of God and his great love for us. Just as a parent to their children, God desires for us to have a wonderful life!

This week we will begin to understand Fellowship, and the enormous desire that God has for a close connectedness with us.

Let your hearts be stirred this week!

Day One: The Importance of Fellowship

Day Two: The Enemy of Fellowship

Day Three: Remaining in Fellowship

Day Four: The Walk of Fellowship

Day Five: Restored Fellowship

Day One

The Importance of Fellowship

Fellowship.

It is the choice word used among Christian circles, to some fellowship indicates the times when some folks get together and talk about churchy things, to others it simply means party time. Yet in God's eyes that is not what fellowship is, and I would wager to say that many of us don't know what God means *when* he speaks about fellowship in his word.

So, what is fellowship, and why is it such an important concept to understand? Better still, why is it important to have fellowship between ourselves and others, and ourselves and God?

To begin we need to go back to the beginning and look at God's design in the garden.

Turn to Genesis 1:26 and read through to 3:24, then answer the questions below:

In whose image was man created? _____
_____

How was Man formed and given life? _____
_____

What did God make to suit Adam? _____
_____

How was Eve presented to Adam? _____
_____

The relationship between God and man was special from the very beginning; it was a relationship distinctly different from the rest of creation. For instance none of the birds, fish, animals, or vegetation were described as bearing God's image, that includes the apes. Mankind *alone* is described as bearing God's image and likeness.

The way in which Adam and Eve were created is much different in description as well. With man God formed him and breathed life into him and with woman God took the rib from Adam and fashioned her.

In describing the creation of man the Bible uses the word "yatsar" which is to "squeeze into shape, mold, as a potter unto clay"[10]. Here we get the picture that our Creator God took a lump of dirt and formed it in his hands until the perfect likeness of himself had been made, and in a moment of joy and pleasure he breathed his life into the empty, lifeless lungs. Adam awakes, and the first thing he sees are the loving eyes of Almighty God.

Then there is woman, who in the same way was sculpted and built in the hands of God, and when she had been stirred to life the Bible says something very sweet.

"Then the Lord God made a woman from the rib he had taken out of the man, and <u>He brought her to man</u>." (Genesis 2:22)

Here you can imagine the first wedding takes place, with the Father walking his daughter down the aisle, and he presents her to man.

Yes, Adam and Eve had a very special relationship with the Lord, however, this relationship did not begin and end with creation. We can know that the fellowship God had intended between himself and mankind was marked by four things.

1. God and Man talked.

> **Read Genesis 3:8-13, mark in the boxes below who was involved in the dialog.**
>
> __ God __ Adam __ Eve

2. God and Man walked

>Read again Genesis 3:8, how can we know from this verse that the garden walk was a normal occurrence?

3. God and Man worked together

>Read Genesis 1:28-30 and 2:8-15, what evidence is there that God and Man worked together?

4. God Provided for Man

>What, according to Genesis 3:21, did God do for Adam and Eve *after* they fell into sin?

As an aside, I find it very interesting that even after such a betrayal as the one perpetrated by Adam and Eve that God made them clothes, he could have said what my Mom used to say: "Don't let the door hit ya where God split ya".

Can you begin to see what fellowship is? <u>It is unity, connectedness, and partnership.</u>

Don't you want a relationship like that with the God of Heaven? Do you believe it is possible?

From the very beginning the design for mankind was to be just like it was between Adam and Eve and their Creator. We have just learned that it was a special relationship, and because God is the Creator we also know that he was the one to initiate the relationship.

That is the same for us! God initiated a relationship with us upon our creation, and though we may have not opened our eyes upon birth to see the Lord we can know that our creation was special too.

Read Psalm 139:14, what does this verse tell you about your creation?

Oh yes, my friend, you were made in a special way to have a special relationship with your Maker.

1st Corinthians 1:9 says that "God, <u>who has called you into fellowship</u> with his Son Jesus Christ our Lord, is faithful". This tells us that God still intends for us to have fellowship with him, through Jesus!

What then is this thing called fellowship and why is it so very important in the life of a believer?

The word fellowship is Koinonia, also Koinonos in Greek, it means "partnership, participation, a sharer, a companion."[11]

Adam and Eve were created for companionship with the Father, they were to share in the rulership of earth, and they were participating in an extraordinarily intimate relationship with the Lord. God was their

Father, they were his beloved children. It's terribly heartbreaking that it ended so badly.

What was the consequence for sinning against God, according to Genesis 3:21-24?

Now read Isaiah 59:1-2, what is the consequence when we sin against God?

Adam and Eve were sent from the Garden, into a barren land which would yield little. They traded in their unified participation with God for weeds and dust and pain, but even worse they lost a connection with God that would never be as it was for they would never again walk in the Garden with their God.

When you and I sin we separate ourselves from God and the connectedness we enjoyed at one time changes.

But we have hope!

Turn to 1st John 1:9 and write the verse below:

We have Jesus, the atonement for our sin; he who stands at the throne interceding on our behalf, restoring us to fellowship.

So, why is fellowship important and why do we need it so badly?

The Eden Design

Because, my friend, that is the way we were made! God built us with a need for Him and this need can only be satiated by Him. It is a need to put ourselves in the hand of he who molded us, our Father.

Jesus said "I tell you the truth, anyone who will not receive the kingdom of God like a little child will never enter into it." (Mark 10:15)

Sometimes it is so easy to convince ourselves that we don't need anyone – especially God, but Jesus said we must come to him as children. Children are the most needy beings in all mankind, there is nothing they can do apart from someone teaching them, loving them, and providing for them.

Can you recognize the truth of this? Do you know that you need fellowship with God?

My friend, when you realize your great need for God it *will* change your life.

This week we will look at different aspects of fellowship; what messes it up, how we stay in fellowship and we'll also look at someone who did it right! I pray that you will come with anticipation to your prayer time today – perhaps you will meet God in a way that you haven't met with him in a long time. As a child.

Day Two

The Enemy of Fellowship

What do you want from life? What are your goals? I'm not talking about work goals, or family goals; no dream vacations, or aspiring actress stuff. I am talking about emotional, deep in the heart goals.

Make a list of these goals.

As humans we have been created to want these things and we all have tried in every way possible to make it happen. Yet we always fall short don't we?

"If I could only make more money then I will be happy…"

"If my kids were more well-behaved then I would have peace in my home…"

"If I could only find the right man then I would be complete…"

Do you notice that in each of these statements above that there is a common word? One simple letter…I.

In the pursuit of our emotional needs and desires we have given birth to a monster. This monster is demanding, selfish, controlling, angry… and at the root of this monstrousity is always the same root, the root of <u>Self.</u>

Now I am not judging you or implying that there is something wrong with wanting to be emotionally fulfilled and happy. Not at all. Do you remember the Eden Design? God has intended for us to have *"abundant life"*, and he certainly desires us to be happy! But you will not be happy in the way God intended it apart from pursuing Christ. Any other kind of pursuit for happiness is striving and it will never end the way you'd hoped.

Remember the story of the Prodigal Son? He left home, having demanded his inheritance, in the pursuit of pleasure and happiness. Read Luke 15:11-24, what happened to him in all of his striving?

All sinful behaviors truly find their rooting in self-centeredness. Let's do a little exercise, search your motives behind your behaviors and fill in the following.

Why do I get Angry?

Why do I buy more than I need?

Why do I brag about my accomplishments?

Why do I demean my accomplishments?

Did you discover that **you** are at the center?

I am blessed to have some dear friends who sat me down one day to tell me that they could see pride in me because of the way that I interacted with them and others. I was so self-focused, yep that's pride, that I would always angle our conversations around me and what was going on in my life and never really care what was going on in their lives. Sadly, because of my pride I had lost a few very close friends. It was very courageous for my friends to point out my sin, in doing so it changed my heart and brought us all into a closer friendship.

This, my friends, is what Jesus is trying to accomplish in your heart! He wants to show you your sinfulness, not to shame you but to change you and to deepen your relationship! What love!

Read Matthew 10:38 and Luke 9:23. What does Jesus say that we must do?

Jesus says it must be our daily mission to die to ourselves. To "put to death whatever belongs to your earthly nature." (Colossians 3:5), and we must take up our cross.

What does that mean to you, to take up your cross?

The cross was a killing weapon. It was a symbol of pain, suffering and humiliation.

Wait a minute.

Does this mean that we are to make ourselves suffer?

In a word…yes.

If my natural self wants only that which satisfies or pleases me than when I choose to deny my sin nature I will suffer.

When I choose to transform an ugly and rugged piece of land into a beautiful and fruitful garden I have to work at it. I risk sunburn, dirty and calloused hands, scratched knees and sore shoulders when I work the ground. However the outcome of all that "suffering" brings me great joy and satisfaction.

It will be the hardest thing that you'll ever do, this dying to self. Oh, but the reward of knowing the peace, feeling the approval and sensing the pleasure of God…

So let's look on the flipside of what we can expect from a self-serving life rather than a self-denying life?

Write the outcomes of a self lived life from each verse.

James 1:13-15

Proverbs 13:10

James 3:16

Fights, darkness, disorder, evil and death. Sounds great, huh?

Being a follower of Christ is really a paradox, we are to do the exact opposite of what makes sense to a lost world. To them "they think it strange that we do not plunge with them into the same flood of dissipation" (1st Peter 4:4) To the lost world it's all about taking care of #1. To us it is living for the true #1, Jesus Christ.

Have you recognized the pros and cons of dying to yourself? Is it clear that the best choice is to be like Jesus and put our desires to death?

Sweet one, I want you to understand that this dying to self thing is something that we have been given the power to do. Read Colossians 3:8 below, circle the word that confirms our involvement in the process.

> *"But now you must rid yourselves of all such things as these: anger, rage, malice, slander and filthy language from your lips."*

You. Your choice. Your decision.

Day Three

Remaining in Fellowship

I had a wild rose bush in my front yard. It was the kind that had thin branches and small flowering rosebuds. The design of this rose bush was for it to climb. In the summer I would take great care to tuck the branches of the rose bush into a trellis, clipping stray branches; it would look beautiful under managed care. However, the summers that my girls were small and it was not as easy to do a lot of outside work I neglected the rose bush. I didn't guide it and prune it the way it needed. It became a very ugly and jumbled mess of branches, leaves and thorns. It spread into the bushes next to it, poked into the siding of my house; its leaves withered and it didn't flower much. It was so out of control that I ended up cutting it down to the ground.

If you know anything about gardening you know that pruning is necessary in order to stimulate new growth, remove diseased or dead branches that inhibit fruit-bearing, and encourage more fruit to grow.

Now think spiritually. What do you think the Lord is trying to encourage when he allows painful circumstances (pruning) to come your way?

I have a brother who went through a very long season of wild living. Drugs, women, parties, and bars were his life. Try as I may I could not seem to help him see the error of his ways and it was definitely an act of God's grace that his life was turned around. God took up his pruning shears on that boy, and it indeed took some serious pruning on God's part; praise be to our Mighty Gardener!

Without mentioning names have you ever known a Christian who was wild, with no direction; one who lives as though they aren't really saved? Has that person been you, is it still? What is this person like?

John 15:1-5
"I am the true vine, and My Father is the vinedresser. 2 "Every branch in Me that does not bear fruit, He takes away; and every branch that bears fruit, He prunes it so that it may bear more fruit. 3 "You are already clean because of the word which I have spoken to you. 4 "Abide in Me, and I in you. As the branch cannot bear fruit of itself unless it abides in the vine, so neither can you unless you abide in Me. 5 "I am the vine, you are the branches; he who abides in Me and I in him, he bears much fruit, for apart from Me you can do nothing. NASU

Read John 15:1-5 in the margin.

According to verse 2 why does the Gardener prune the branch? What can you do if you don't remain with Jesus, based on verse 4?

Do you understand from these verses that God prunes us in order that we would bear fruit, and that we can't bear fruit if we don't remain with Jesus.

This for me raises a very big question: *In practical terms what does it look like when God begins to prune?*

The Eden Design | 123

Practical Pruning --- *It is painful*

Read 2nd Corinthians 4:17 below:

> *"For our light and momentary troubles are achieving for us an eternal glory that far outweighs them all."*

It *is* a hard thing to be pruned, sometimes it is embarrassing, sometimes devastating, and most of the time it is heartbreaking! But it is *so* necessary.

When God prunes us he may show us an attitude, a behavior, perhaps a stronghold that needs to go.

Turn to Hebrews 12: 4-11, what does God's discipline produce?

Did you notice that it did not say that God's discipline produces robots? We are not disciplined for the purpose of shame and dejection any more than a good parent would want to shame and humiliate their children. No, we are disciplined to produce a harvest…to become more like Jesus; more love, more faith, more maturity!

That's pretty cool.

So, based on God's love and desire for harvests, what does pruning look like in practical terms?

Consider some examples from the well-known Bible stories of old.

Match the Pruning tool with the Bible stories:

The prodigal son   A. Persecution
(Luke 15:11-20)_____

David's Crimes   B. Allow believer to self-destruct
(2nd Samuel 12:1-7)_____

The Fiery Furnace   C. Conviction from Holy Spirit
(Daniel 3:19-27)_____

Paul's Conversion   D. Confrontation by others
(Acts 22:6-10)_____

The ways our Lord worked in the lives of these people is not an all-inclusive list of how God works; not all of your experiences may be as dramatic as those of these Biblical figures, but I am certain they've been just as effective.

I experienced a painful pruning in college. I was going to a private college and was working several jobs in order to reduce my debt load. At the same time I was dating a young man who lived long distance from me. One of my jobs was as a janitor in the teacher's offices where I had access to phones from which I would make "free" long distance phone calls to this boyfriend of mine. I was deceitful and I was stealing from the college.

Not long after I began making my phone calls I was confronted by my boss who promptly fired me. I then had to appear before the lady in charge of student affairs and confess to her my crimes. It was this woman who pointed out to me that because of the many jobs I was holding I had not made it to church in months and my spiritual fervor for the Lord had greatly waned. I had never before connected my spiritual complacency with the ease of choosing a sinful path! God chose to use the Pruning Tool of confrontation with me. It hurt a lot; but I began to grow again after it happened.

My friend, do not fear pruning from the Lord. Embrace it, because you know it is the working hand of a loving God in your life. It is necessary for God to mold our lives so that we can remain in fellowship with him. It is during those hard times of discipline and pruning that we can look to God for our strength and our growth…what a blessing!

Day Four

The Walk of Fellowship

Having grown up in church I was well acquainted with the lingo of the local church. I speak fluent "Christianese", if you will.

An example of church lingo would be, "Oh you have got to pray for Sue, she is doing….", which could be translated to say "Guess what Sue has been up to..". Another example of Christianese is "how is your walk with God going?"

Of course the down pat answer is "oh, just fine thanks." The question however is a really important question that we as brothers and sisters in Christ should be asking. And when the question is asked it should be no surprise to the asker if they have to settle in for a long conversation! Seriously, if you come to me asking how my walk is going or how I am doing I'm gonna assume you really want to know!

What does it mean to walk with God? After this lesson it is my hope that your walk with God will take on a whole new meaning.

<u>The Enoch Walk</u>

There is a man of the old testament who was apparently a very important figure. He is often overlooked, however, because his name is mentioned only three times in the whole Bible. His name is Enoch. Enoch walked with God.

Let's read about Enoch and then we will explore why he is so important to us today.

Turn in your bible and read the following:

Genesis 5:21-24   Hebrews 11:5-6   Jude 1:14-15

Based on the verses what is your first impression of Enoch?

Of the thousands of figures recorded in the history of the Bible very few are recorded as having walked with God. Though the initial impression of walking with another seems trite the idea of *walking with* another really is a very big concept.

When you go for walks what kind of people do you walk with?

If I am going to go on a walk it's going to be with someone I like, or at the very least am acquainted with, not often do I walk with a stranger, unless I am showing them where the bathroom is at in the mall. You walk with friends, you walk with family.

What do you do as you walk along together?

I know these questions seem a little, well, duh. Here is the point: God desires to take walks with us. When my husband and I were still dating we would take long walks together, holding hands and dreaming about the future. It was a time of intimacy for us in our budding relationship. God wants to take long, slow walks with us as well; he wants to spend time with us in our moments of prayer, study, and meditation. More than that, God desires us to have a *lifestyle* of walking with him.

In the amplified Bible Enoch's walk with God is described as habitual fellowship. We'll see later that this type of walk was very pleasing to our God.

So what is required for us to walk in habitual fellowship with God?

1. **We must be saved.**

This may seem obvious, yet the word of God tells us that there will be those who face Jesus at the throne of Judgment saying "Lord, Lord, did we not prophesy in your name, and in your name drive out demons and perform many miracles? Then I will tell them plainly, 'I never knew you. Away from me, you evildoers!'" (Matt. 7:22)

If you have not been saved, not only are you <u>not</u> walking *with* God, you are walking *away* from God.

2. **We must be purposeful**

Read again Hebrews 11:5-6. Verse 5 speaks of Enoch, who we know walked with God and we know he *pleased* God. So, in verse 6 what is it we are to do to please God?

Did you see it? We must have *faith* to please God and faith comes from believing that he is (exists) and from earnestly seeking him!

In order to walk with God in habitual fellowship we must make it a lifestyle to seek to know him, to know his ways and to please him through our actions and thoughts and words.

Read James 4:4 and write it below:

My friend, we simply can't walk with God and the world at the same time.

3. **We must follow God's course**

Here comes the faith building part of our walk, because sometimes God walks into valleys that we would rather avoid! I have heard in

The Eden Design | 129

prayers, and in fact prayed this way myself "Lord please walk with me through my day…" The problem here is that He is not walking with us, <u>we</u> are walking with <u>him</u>.

David understood this concept quite well. Read about that in Psalms 23:1-4; circle below the descriptive words that imply God's leadership over the walk he was on with David.

> The Lord is my shepherd,
> I shall not want.
> 2 He makes me lie down in green pastures;
> He leads me beside quiet waters.
> 3 He restores my soul;
> He guides me in the paths of righteousness
> For His name's sake.
> 4 Even though I walk through the valley of the shadow of death,
> I fear no evil, for You are with me;
> Your rod and Your staff, they comfort me
> NASU

Isn't it wonderful to know that God isn't hurrying along his path yelling over his shoulder at us, "come on, keep up!".

No, he guides, he leads, he comforts.

Here's something to think about: when you are facing a decision do you pray and wait for the Lord to lead, or do you charge ahead ripping open doors along the way?

4. We must continue walking

The bible does not say that Enoch had <u>a</u> walk with God, it says that he walked with God. He did it all the time; it was a daily, ongoing walk. We cannot expect that we can walk with God today but tomorrow just do as we please.

Jesus addresses this issue; the "I will follow you if…" and the "I will follow you when…" problem that we Christians have.

Read in Luke 9:57-62; what excuses did they come up with for not following Jesus at once?

In the NIV verse 57 says, "as they walked along"; Jesus is always about the Father's business, he is always on the go. He wasn't about to stop for these men who were willing to follow him if…It is our job to see where the Lord is working and to walk with him there, don't expect him to hold the universe for you.

If you really want to walk with the Lord you must do it – now.

As I wrote at the beginning of today's lesson Enoch was mentioned little in the pages of scripture, yet he was an important example to those of us who want to walk in fellowship with our God.

His example shows us that:

He had God's pleasure

> "Before he was taken, the Scripture says that he was a man who truly pleased God." Hebrews 11:5

He had God's insight

> "Enoch, the seventh from Adam _prophesied_ about these men" Jude 14

He had God's unique retirement plan

"Enoch walked with God; one day Enoch could not be found, because God took him." Genesis 5:24

At the end of my life I hope that I will be considered as one who pleased God – what a fantastic tribute to a man who spent his days at the side of his God.

Day Five

Restored Fellowship

Sweet friend we have made it to the end of another week. I am so glad that you are hanging in there and I pray for you that you are taking God's word and sowing it deeply in your heart. Today we will be skipping around the Bible a lot, we have so much to learn! So roll up your sleeves and let's dig in to this treasure chest!

God created Adam and Eve to be sinless. When they were created without sin they had unhindered intimacy and perfect fellowship with their Creator. It was as God intended.

It was good.

Then sin came, and along with sin came brokenness. Broken intimacy, broken fellowship, broken hearts.

We have been learning about God's design for fellowship; what hinders us, what should motivate us. Something we need to learn now is that our fellowship with God can be good, but it will never be perfectly restored this side of Heaven.

We ebb and flow with our sinful struggles, and our fellowship with God is caught in the crossfire.

But this fact should give us great hope! We have that hope that when we get to heaven our relationship with Jesus will be beautiful, perfect.

So what's the point of working so hard against this world to have a good walk with God if it can't even be a perfect relationship.

Think about that...do you have any relationship in your life right now that is perfect?

Unless you are really *lying* to yourself I would wager to say that you all answered no. NO relationship is perfect; not with your kids, not with your spouse, not with your friends. So would you work any less hard on your relationship with them?

All relationships fall victim to this fallen world in its imperfection, but with God we have the hope of restoration fellowship. Restoration fellowship is the relationship we will have when we are no longer enslaved by this sin nature. We will know the Lord completely and intimately. As John said "we will see him as he is!" (see 1st John 3:2)

Of all people you would think that when Jesus walked this Earth that he would have had perfect relationships that were fulfilling and wonderful. You would think that his disciples would have been the least selfish, most enduring sorts who knew Jesus throughout! After all they had the Almighty God with them 24/7, shouldn't they have represented restoration fellowship?

See for yourself:

Read John 14:5-9, Did Philip have a restoration fellowship with Jesus? Why or why not?

Now read Luke 22:54-62, did Peter have restoration fellowship with Jesus? Why or why not?

Finally, read Luke 22:24, when was it the disciples were having their discussion and what was it about?

They were arguing over who would be the best while at the Lord's Supper! Jesus' serious words of his eminent death, his betrayal, his desire to share the supper again in the kingdom were met by "Dude, I bet I'm gonna be the best in the kingdom.." and "Nu-uh! I think *I'm* going to be the best!"

It reminds me of the times I would be talking seriously to my oldest daughter about needing salvation, or being kind to her sisters, and she would very seriously reply: "Mommy you have a booger in your nose."

Something that was off with my daughter, as with the disciples, was the mature knowledge that we need to have the relationship, the authority, the life giving message that Jesus gives! We *need this relationship* but our egos, our selfishness, gets in the way.

Oh I long for the day when I stand sinless and renewed before my Savior. I long for the day of a restored fellowship that my ego can't get in the way of!

Look again at Peter's denial. Skim through Luke 22:54-62, looking especially at verse 61. Write verse 61 below:

Now read Luke 22:31-32

Peter's betrayal of his relationship with Jesus was just as acute as Judas' betrayal. Jesus knew Peter's denials were coming, he knew that Peter would abandon their fellowship.

Jesus also knows that we will abandon him. When we sin we cause broken fellowship, and when we willfully sin we are no better than Judas and Peter. The difference between Judas and Peter was the condition of their hearts. Judas felt bad and killed himself but was he repentant? Peter sobbed his eyeballs out in repentance. Jesus knew this would be the case, so to Peter Jesus said, "And when you have turned back, strengthen your brothers." (verse 32)

He says that to us as well.

Have you abandoned the Lord? Have you returned yet?

When I was a little girl I hoped I would grow up and get married. When I was a young woman I hoped the young man I had just met would be "the one". When we were engaged I hoped the wedding would be the stuff of dreams. On my wedding day I hoped that I would be as happy for the rest of my life as I was on that day.

So much hope. Our lives are based on hopes, filled with hopes. We were created to hope. Hope for happiness, hope for fulfillment, hope for completion.

….and one day we will stand before the Lord. The culmination of all of life's hopes.

> *"No longer will there be any curse…they will see his face, and his name will be on their foreheads. There will be no more night. They will not need the light of a lamp or the light of the sun, for the Lord God will give them light. And they will reign forever and ever." Revelation 22:3-5*

"And I heard a loud voice from the throne saying, 'now the dwelling of God is with men, and he will live with them. They will be his people, and God himself will be with them and be their God. He will wipe every tear from their eyes. There will be no more death or mourning or crying or pain, for the old order of things has passed away.'" Revelation 21:3-4

I can't wait. I can't wait to see Jesus, to touch him, to hug him, to bow at his feet with my face lifted. To have my King wipe the last tears from my eyes and whisper "Welcome home."

That is fellowship restored.

WEEK SIX

Design: Fulfillment

Here we are, in the season of harvest. We have planted seeds, cared for the new growth, pulled the weeds, and watered it well. Now is the time to finish strong as this week we get to see the beauty of God's Eden design.

Day One:	A Need for Fulfillment
Day Two:	A Fulfilled Thirst
Day Three:	A Fulfilled Purpose
Day Four:	A Fulfilling Joy
Day Five:	Oaks of Righteousness

Day One

A Need for Fulfillment

Nothing drains me of my energy more than when I am dehydrated. I get cranky, really cranky. Ask my husband and I am sure he will give a big Amen to that one! There have been times when I have felt myself getting dehydrated and I basically freak out needing a drink of water immediately; I have had to pay upwards of $3.00 for water because my thirst was so consuming!

Have you ever experienced a thirst that demanded immediate quenching? What did that feel like?

When I am thirsty I am almost irrational, I feel weak, slumped. Just like a flower begins to look when it needs watering; that is how I feel… withered.

It is the same way when our spirit is thirsty. When we haven't gone to God with our worries, our concerns and our sins we truly begin to wilt.

Read about David's thirst in Psalm 42:1-2. Do you remember a time when you thirsted for God?

Do you notice David's question in the second half of verse 2? He says "when can I go and meet with God?" That reminds me of when my daughters say "when is my Daddy coming home?"

Just as my daughters longs to see their Daddy, so too David longed for his time with the Father because he knew that it is God alone who can quench our thirst!

What is it that causes such thirst? What is it about mankind that we seem to have such a need for the filling that God offers? Every person on the face of the Earth has a need for God, a longing that unbelievers can't explain, and that is why there is so much agony!

What are things that people do, apart from God, to fill their need within them?

Teenagers have premarital sex to try to fill the need, housewives have emotional affairs with romance novels and movies to try to fill the need, people turn to alcohol, drugs, shopping, food, and horoscopes – all these things just to fill their need.

Let's look at a conversation that Jesus had with a woman who tried in vain to fill her own neediness.

Turn to John 4:7-26; based on these verses what was it this woman tried to fill herself up with?

This poor woman went from one man to another, from one failed relationship to another, looking to be filled. Notice in verse 16 that Jesus addressed her failed attempts at self fulfillment by pointing out the nature of her need. At first I found it odd that she would ask for the living water and he would bring up her, but Jesus knew that her request for the living water wasn't for the real living water, it was just another quick fix. Jesus had to reveal to her the depth of her sin and the depth of her need for fulfillment before she could truly ask to be filled.

What is it that you do to try to fill your own cup? Is it working?

Being in the fitness industry for so long I have learned a number of things about exercise and nutrition, proper hydration being one of those lessons. One of the things that I have learned is that sometimes when people are thirsty they don't know that they are thirsty! Their body tries to tell them that it needs water but because they are not dialed in to their physical symptoms they end up eating something instead. They feel a need and assume they are hungry, yet the whole time what they needed was water.

Many believers are clueless about their spiritual thirst, they are not dialed in to their symptoms. They begin to fill themselves with things they hope will bring satisfaction when what they really need is a fulfilling connection with God.

Oh, that we would recognize within ourselves the insatiable need for our God! He alone can satisfy the longings that we have in our hearts; this being such an important topic we will continue along the same lines tomorrow.

In the meantime spend some time in prayer asking the Lord to reveal where you have a thirst for Him that you have not recognized or have tried to satisfy it without him.

Day Two

A Fulfilled Thirst

Yesterday we talked about our need for water, for Living Water. We each have a need in our lives, an emptiness, that we try to fill with temporal things. This need creates a thirst and once we can begin to recognize that the thirst we have is a need for God we can begin to draw from the well of God.

As a reminder, read John 4:10-14. In the first half of verse 10 Jesus responds to the Samaritan woman in a rather peculiar manner. Write his response below:

Rather than responding to her question of "how can you ask me for a drink?" with an "I'm thirsty, that's why" Jesus begins to reveal to her *who* he is. He very clearly told the Samaritan woman "I am the source". It is Jesus alone who can fill the need, the emptiness within us. Christ alone, yes Christ alone.

I am reminded of a song, you may recognize it as well..

> *In Christ alone, I place my trust, and find my glory in the power of the cross, in every victory let it be said of me – my source of strength, my source of hope is Christ alone.* [12]

In John 4:13-14 Jesus tells us where to go with our need. He says "whoever drinks the water I give him will never thirst, indeed the water I give him will become in him a spring of water welling up to eternal life."

So why are believers so thirsty?! Is Jesus saying that if you drink the water he offers it would be a one time cure for emotional turmoil and hardships within your soul? If so, why are so many believers dried out?

There is so much we could worry about and be anxious about. There is so much that we desire, so many needs! We women have big needs; big emotional needs. Do you know what I'm saying? We need to know that we are taken care of, that we are wanted and needed. We want to know that we are loved and that someone will be there to rescue us when we are in trouble.

Every woman feels this way, so it must be something that God created within us. This need for deep filling.

Jesus knows that we have this need for fulfillment. He also knows that fulfillment can't be achieved apart from a relationship with him.

It is when we try to achieve our own fulfillment that we dry up. We must begin to recognize our soul thirst!

Read Matthew 11:28, what is necessary for us to do in order to receive rest from our burdens? Why is it so hard to do?

It seems so simple. "Come to me!" Admit to yourself that you can't do this all by yourself and come to me! Tell me your burdens, pour out your heart to me, cry yourself to sleep in my arms and I will give you rest. Doesn't that sound amazing?

David knew his deep soul thirst, and he knew where to go with it.

The Eden Design | 145

> *"From the ends of the earth I call to you, I call as my heart grows faint; Lead me to the rock that is higher than I."*
> *(Psalm 61:2)*

The Samaritan woman was a woman much like us, with a deep soul thirst she had for so long filled with all the wrong things. Jesus' words to her are for us as well, because his living water is for each of us.

> *"But whoever drinks of the water I give him will never thirst. Indeed, the water I give him will become in him a spring of water welling up to eternal life."*
> *John 4:14*

The word "drink" in the Greek is "pino" meaning "a prolonged form of pio, which is to drink."[13] Get that? A prolonged form!

My friend, if you have found yourself with a perpetual soul thirst than you are forgetting to drink from the well. Drink it, drink it and drink it some more! Soak in it until you get prunie!

To answer the question from before as to why believers are so dried out you should look again at God's design. Are you dried out because you have neglected to be obedient? Have you forgotten the importance of daily intimacy with our Savior? Have you overlooked the character of God and placed him on a little shelf where you can take him out at your leisure?

Perhaps you are trying so hard to fulfill yourself that you cannot hear the gentle wooing of the Holy Spirit saying "come!"

Write below each of God's Eden designs for us:

_____

_____

_____

_____

Now go back and circle the one that you need most right now. Sweet girl, you need to go to the rock that is higher than yourself. Ask him to fulfill you so you can taste and see that the Lord is good!

Day Three

A Fulfilling Joy

Sometimes life is really hard.

People die, marriages end, jobs are lost.

Then we are told to buck up! Lift your chin! Think happy thoughts.... pretend that nothing is wrong because life is supposed to be happy (insert cheesy grin).

If you ask someone what the goal of life is the answer would most likely be "to be happy". But this is a fallen world where the results of disobedience takes its toll; a world of death and tears.

How can a woman be happy if her marriage is a disaster, how can she be happy if she has to face *another* miscarriage, how can a woman be happy if she can't find a decent man to settle down with and raise a family.

Yet we are told we're supposed to be happy.

The funny thing is, though, that you will not find word one in the word of God that our jobs as humans are to be happy. "Thou shalt be happy" has never been commanded by God. It is, if you will, a self-imposed standard that this world has fixed in our minds; "no matter what make yourself happy."

It is the unconditional pursuit of happiness that has caused the ruination of so many:

"This marriage does not make me happy, so it's over!"

"This job does not make me happy, so I quit!"

"This baby will ruin my chances at future happiness so…"

Do you see how this striving for happiness is really a drive for self-fulfillment which is, essentially, incredibly selfish.

Is this part of God's design?

Do you think God cares about your happiness?   Yes   No

Dear friend, God does care for your happiness. He loves you so completely that he concerns himself with every part of your life, especially your happiness! But God wants more for you than mere happiness; he wants you to have joy!

In the Greek Joy is "Chara", also "Chairo" meaning calmly happy, calm delight, cheerfulness, gladness, exceeding joy.[14]

This word carries with it the idea of one who at the end of her life sits in her rocking chair with a delightful little smile, and a sigh of contentment. It is the underlying sense that no matter what happens in your life you can lean back and say, "yeah, it's good."

Joy is the feeling we have when a relationship is restored, it is the joy we feel when our children do something kind to another. It is the feeling we have when all is well.

Here lies the beauty of God's design –indeed he wants us to be fulfilled; lacking nothing. Yet this is not a thing we can achieve for ourselves. Our lives were meant to be so intertwined with the heart of God that the act of loving the Creator would bring us unspeakable joy. We need the Father.

The prospect of the righteous is joy, but the hopes of the wicked come to nothing. Prov. 10:28

Read Proverbs 10:28 in the margin; what is the prospect of the righteous?

Who are they that are righteous? Are they not the ones who fear the Lord, respecting his authority and obeying him? Are they not the ones who understand that they are tiny specks of dust in the hands of the

One who formed the sun? And are they not the same ones who know that "the prospect of the righteous is joy."

We are the apple of the Father's eye. We are called his children, and are the display of his splendor.

Turn to Zephaniah 3:17 and write this verse below:

You see, our God takes great delight in you! Would he not then desire your joy?

It is a very difficult concept for our "just do it" generation to grasp; the concept that we can not make ourselves as happy as God can make us, because we want it now, on our terms, in our way!

But joy is not about making ourselves happy, it can't be achieved through selfish pursuits. Joy happens when our lives bring pleasure to the Father. Oh that is my constant prayer, that I would please the Father since I know that when I feel his pleasure resting on me – oh, that's joy.

Think of a small child. They are often so eager to help Mommy, or to draw her pictures, or to pick her flowers. "Look Mommy I did this for you!" and the *joy* they feel when Mommy reaches down and scoops them up and cries "How wonderful, it is the best gift ever!"

That is the joy we really need.

Read Matthew 25:21; What was the servant being praised for? What does the servant get to share with his master?

The servant was obedient, he had been faithful to his master while the master had been away. Now he is rewarded by sharing in the joy and happiness of a delighted King.

Read Psalm 37:3-5 below and circle the action words:

> *Trust in the Lord and do good; Dwell in the land and enjoy safe pasture. Delight yourself in the Lord and he will give you the desires of your heart. Commit your way to the Lord; Trust in him and he will do this"*

Is it hard for you to trust the Lord to supply your needs and desires? Why?

Do you believe that your faithfulness to God will result in joy?

Life is very hard, yet we must remember that we have a God who is the Most High God, the Almighty King, the Lord of Lords. Our Creator, our Father, our Friend. We must learn to <u>trust</u> him, we must learn to <u>depend</u> on Him, and learn to <u>hear his voice</u> by knowing his word.

It is then that we experience his joy because all those worries, all that striving for happiness…it's gone.

> "Blessed (happy) is the man who does not walk in the counsel of the wicked or stand in the way of sinners or sit in the seat of mockers. But his **delight** is in the law of the Lord, and on his law he meditates day and night. He is like a tree planted by streams of

water…For the Lord watches over the way of the righteous but the way of the wicked will perish."

Psalm 1:1-3,6

My friend, let God be your joy and your delight that you may have a very fulfilling joy.

Day Four

A Fulfilled Purpose

Oh the wonders of our matchless God, he who desires to give us life, abundant, joyful and fulfilled. Our King who cares so deeply for his servants, who came to restore us to a relationship with the Father. He who did not leave us abandoned as orphans – hopeless, homeless; no, he sent the Holy Spirit as the divine tour guide through this life.

What a Mighty God we serve! Don't you agree?

It is my prayer for you, my friend, that God won't simply be a back-of-the mind after thought, but that he will be the forethought, the check point for every decision that you make in life.

This of course brings us to our lesson for today.

Have you ever wondered what your purpose in life is? Do you feel like you know what your purpose is, if so what is it?

I know a few teenagers who believe that their purpose is to grow up and be foreign missionaries, and they are already taking steps to train themselves as missionaries. They are going on summer missions trips, starting Bible studies in their schools, all because they believe that God has called them there.

To those girls I say, "I am totally jealous!!!". I absolutely believe that God can call folks to ministry at early ages and he keeps them unwavering. I, however, had no clue what God was going to do in my life or with my life – nope, no clue. I had an inkling of being called to ministry when I was 9 years old but I veered on and off that course throughout the remainder of my youth. I changed my major five times throughout my college career, settling on recreation management because it seemed fun and would be easy to finish within the four years.

All the while I felt directionless, purposeless, aiming to make my way through this life ending up as happy as possible. Floundering, flailing in a rough ocean of aimlessness.

Where are you right now: are you flailing or are you marching down a marked path?

Here is where we begin to learn about the beauty of God's design. He never meant for us to lack purpose, nor to feel lost and confused about life.

Now this may seem over simplified but let me lay out for you the purpose of life for every single individual on the face of this earth: We are to bring glory to God!

Read Isaiah 61:3 below and underline what this verse says is your purpose.

> "…to bestow of them a crown of beauty instead of ashes, the oil of gladness instead of mourning, and a garment of praise instead of a spirit of despair. They will be called Oaks of Righteousness, a planting of the Lord for the display of His splendor."

Our purpose? To display God's splendor! The King James Version says it this way: "..the planting of the Lord, that he might be glorified."

We are a planting that the Almighty Gardener has placed in a specific place in a specific season so that **if** we allow ourselves to step up to our purpose, we will grow into a thing of such beauty that others can not help but know God.

Now, this is the BIG picture.

If you will, the purpose of bringing God glory is the large circle of our life. As I mentioned above, it is the core purpose for every living person on this earth – why do you think so many are walking around as if blind? It is because they are living for bringing glory to themselves instead of bringing glory to their Creator.

So now I am sure you are probably wondering what you can do to fulfill this purpose placed within you. I am sure some of you are wanting a ten point plan of operation, huh?

To begin, we all have to identify the problem; the problem is that we have been asking the wrong question all along! We keep asking "What is *my purpose* in life?" when instead we should be asking "How can I work where God is working to bring Him glory?"

Underline from these verses whose purpose will be fulfilled:

> *"Many are the plans in a man's heart, but it is the Lord's purpose that will prevail." Proverbs 19:21*

> *The Lord will fulfill his purpose for me; your love, O Lord, endures forever – do not abandon the work of your hands." Ps. 138:8*

Doesn't that just make you wonder what God's purpose is? What is God's purpose for mankind, why did he create us in the first place?

I hope by now that answer is easy to answer. Relationship; it all boils down to a relationship with God Almighty.

God designed us for relationship and he has been spending the last 6000 years repairing what our sin nature continues to destroy. How wonderful that God's purpose is for our benefit!

So, we have the big picture that we are to bring God glory, now we can begin to see how God gives us many opportunities to do just that! He has placed within you, my friend, the gifts and talents and abilities to bring Him glory; we only have to recognize it!

Read Ephesians 4:11-13 and 1st Corinthians 12:27-28 and summarize the verses below:

What talents and abilities do *you* possess and how can you use them to bring God glory?

So many are wasting their talents on things that don't matter, ignorantly spending them on behalf of themselves. For a while this may satisfy and feel good, but ultimately our souls are hungry to please God…all else is striving.

In my life I know that the Lord has given me the big picture purpose of bringing Him glory. I also know that he has blessed me with various gifts and talents. For a long time I used to sit in my house and think glumly, "how can God possibly use me? I am a stay at home mom, I don't see people very often…so God must not have a purpose for me."

The thing is, in this season that *is* His purpose for me. I am to glorify God in the raising of my children! Are you an office worker? A church worker? A college student? <u>Then in all that you do bring Glory to our Creator!</u>

What does that look like? It is the inside circle of our ultimate purpose… it is our task at hand, given us by a gracious God, so that we can display his splendor.

Look now at some examples of individuals who had been given a clear task to their lives. See if you can identify what their tasks were and how that worked towards God's purposes and His glory.

Abraham (Genesis 12:1-3)

Isaiah (Isaiah 6:8-13)

Jesus (John 3:14-17)

Abraham and Isaiah were mere men like us; they were told by the Lord what their big circle purpose was – bring Him glory. Then they were given a smaller circle task: for Abraham he was to leave his home and prepare to be the Father of a Great Nation. Isaiah was told to preach repentance to Israel. Do you suppose that once the task was given them Abraham and Isaiah knew each and every day just what to do?

Nope. They, like you and I, had to depend on the Father to guide each step they took or else one day they would lift their head and look around and say, "where am I?"

Psalm 119:105 says "Your word is a lamp unto my feet and a light to my path."

Circle below what a lamp is used for:

To give a grand and glaring light that one can see for miles

Or

To give a gentle glow to a small room

The writer of this psalm used the word lamp, not the word lighthouse! We must walk each day in the light that the Lord has given us for the day.

If you know the story of Abraham you may well know that he strayed from the lamp lit path Almighty God gave him several times. When that happened did Abraham give up on the purpose and task God had set before him? Not at all! He humbly returned to the intimacy and fellowship that awaited him on the gently lit path.

Jesus knew his big circle purpose, and he knew well the task that was set before him that would bring about God's glory. Yet, prior to his ministry years Jesus was not important to his culture, he was not a celebrity, nor was he a person of significance. When Jesus called his disciples they weren't popular, important men either. Yet all of history recognizes the name of Jesus and the names of Peter, James, and Paul. All those who have made a difference in the kingdom didn't do so because of their bank account or their social status – no, they made a difference because they spent their lives glorifying God.

The mission statement of Jesus Christ's life can be summed up in John 17:1-5, read it with me below:

> *Father, the time has come. Glorify your Son, that your Son may glorify you. For you granted him authority over all people that might give eternal life to all those you have given him. Now this is eternal life: that they may know you, the only true God, and Jesus Christ, whom you have sent. I have brought you glory on earth by completing the work you gave me to do. And now, Father, glorify me in your presence with the glory I had with you before the world began."*

We have each been given a purpose and a task. For everyone the task is different, our gifts and talents and personalities are different; but our purpose is universal: bring Glory to God!

In the space below draw a big circle. Inside the big circle draw a smaller circle. Within the small circle write a task that God has given you to complete, and around the outside of the small circle write down some gifts and talents that the Lord has given you in order to complete the task. Finally, around the outside of the big circle write down your ultimate purpose. If you are totally lost just look at my example to guide you.

Writing   Imagination
Supportive husband
Teaching

Raise children
Teach Bible

What now do we do with this insight? Now that we know that we are to glorify God through all things, that we are to work to bring God glory by ministering to others, and that we are to let God reveal what work he will have for us to do based on the gifts he has given us.

We are to wait.

Oh stink. You didn't like that answer did you?

David waited almost 20 years before he became king.

Abraham waited almost 25 years before he was given a son.

The Eden Design | 159

Jesus waited 33 years before he could culminate his life's purpose with his death and resurrection.

Wait on God. Wait for Him to open doors.

In the mean time begin to fulfill your purpose, the highest purpose…. Bring God Glory.

Day Five

Oaks of Righteousness

We have come so far together! For six weeks now we have been exploring the truths of God's gracious design and intent for our lives. I hope that you will have come from this study with more than increased "head knowledge" of our God, but that you will have increased heart knowledge too.

We must always remember that God has created our lives to be more and to have more, and to love more than we could possibly imagine. As my Pastor says, "If God had a middle name, it would be More."

Review the Eden design with me now. In the spaces below write the five things that God has designed for us to enjoy, also write what each one means to you now:

1.

2.

3.

4.

5.

Remember that familiar verse: "I have come that you may have life and have it to the full." (John 10:10). Jesus talks about that full and "more" life that each of us desires. Have you learned to identify what is off in your life and your walk with God that may have caused you to miss the abundant life? Write it below.

If you have recognized a void what is your action plan for change? Pray and ask the Lord what you need to do next, and write below what he reveals.

I pray that each day you will seek the Savior. I pray that you will willfully place yourself at his feet, under his guidance, and put your desires on the cross. When you deny yourself you give the opening that Jesus needs to sweep in and rescue you!

Let's spend the rest of this lesson enjoying the hope that our obedience gives us. Read all of Isaiah chapter 61. Take a careful look at verses 1-3. Here we have Jesus in action; this is what he does for us. Now write all those action verbs below, what will Jesus do?

He is our preacher, our giver of freedom, our comforter – and so much more! Doesn't that deserve a hallelujah right there!

And then there is us. We are written right into scripture; the results of our allowing Jesus to free us, comfort us, save us.

Don't fool yourself friend. The whole of scripture is an if/then statement. Our obedience will cause a heavenly response. Likewise our disobedience and indifference will cause a heavenly response.

Here is heaven's response to our obedience:

"They will be called oaks of righteousness, a planting of the Lord for the display of his splendor. They will rebuild the ancient ruins and restore the places long devastated; they will renew the cities that have been devastated for generations." Along with the beauty for ashes, and garment of praise instead of despair we will bring glory to God the Most High. El Elyon.

Do you remember what that means? What does it mean to you when I say you will bring glory to God?

Our lives reflect God, and the reflection we give off will either lift up His name and his reputation – or it will tarnish it. But when we live lives of obedience and faith our roots will go so deep and we will grow so tall that others can't help but notice that something is different, that we are mighty trees while they are sickly saplings. And when they ask what has caused us to be so we answer on behalf of the Lord our God and we bring Him glory and display *His splendor*.

Then our families will notice.

Those ancient ruins? Those places long devastated? Are they not the generations of our loved ones who are in captivity to sin!

What does God say we can be a part of when we are his oaks of righteousness, regarding our families?

I don't know about you but I have plenty within my family who need to be restored, renewed, and rebuilt. What about you? List their names below:

I feel so moved, so blessed when I think of all that God has in store for my life. Don't you?

God, in his perfect and infinite plan, has designed an Eden within each of our lives. A life of freedom, a life of intimacy, a life of ready obedience, a life of fellowship, and a life a fulfillment. He did not create us to drag us through the mud and bide our time until heaven, he came to give life; abundantly and blessedly more life.

You know now. You know what you need to do, what attitudes you need to dig up and destroy, and what priorities need to be changed in order to cultivate your soil for God's work and God's blessings. So, what are you going to do?

> *"For as the soil makes the sprout come up and a garden causes seed to grow, so the Sovereign Lord will make righteousness and praise spring up before all nations."*
> *Isaiah 61:11*

(ENDNOTES)

1. James Strong, from the *Greek Dictionary of the Exhaustive Concordance of the Bible* (Nashville: Thomas Nelson Publishers), 70.

2. R. Patrick Abergel, M.D., http://www.doctorabergel.com/dermatology/skin_cancer.html

3. James Strong, from the *Greek Dictionary of the Exhaustive Concordance of the Bible* (Nashville: Thomas Nelson Publishers), 66.

4. Webster, *New Webster's Dictionary* (Weston Florida: Paradise Press, Inc), 76

5. James Strong, from the *Hebrew and Aramaic Dictionary of the Exhaustive Concordance of the Bible* (Nashville: Thomas Nelson Publishers),53

6. James Strong, from the *Hebrew and Aramaic Dictionary of the Exhaustive Concordance of the Bible* (Nashville: Thomas Nelson Publishers), 92

7. James Strong, from the *Greek Dictionary of the Exhaustive Concordance of the Bible* (Nashville: Thomas Nelson Publishers),56

8. James Strong, from the *Greek Dictionary of the Exhaustive Concordance of the Bible* (Nashville: Thomas Nelson Publishers), 36, 76.

9. James Strong, from the *Greek Dictionary of the Exhaustive Concordance of the Bible* (Nashville: Thomas Nelson Publishers), 67

10. James Strong, from the *Hebrew and Aramaic Dictionary of the Exhaustive Concordance of the Bible* (Nashville: Thomas Nelson Publishers), 59.

11. James Strong, from the *Greek Dictionary of the Exhaustive Concordance of the Bible* (Nashville: Thomas Nelson Publishers), 50.

12. Michael English, *"In Christ Alone"*, Warner Brothers, 1992.

13. James Strong, from the *Greek Dictionary of the Exhaustive Concordance of the Bible* (Nashville: Thomas Nelson Publishers), 71.

14. James Strong, from the *Greek Dictionary of the Exhaustive Concordance of the Bible* (Nashville: Thomas Nelson Publishers), 98.

ABOUT THE AUTHOR

Christina Jarvie is a wife, mother of three and an impassioned student of God's Word. Her greatest desire is to teach the Word and to serve the Body of Christ and she has done so as an author, worship leader, Bible study teacher and conference speaker. Christina lives in Spokane, Washington raising her children and teaching fitness classes.